POLYMER CLAY JEWELRY

DEBBIE JACKSON

NORTH LIGHT BOOKS
CINCINNATI, OHIO
www.artistsnetwork.com

ABOUT THE AUTHOR

Artist and educator Debbie Jackson has been working with polymer clay for about ten years. She graduated from Miami University (Ohio) with a degree in art education. Debbie is retired from the Columbus Recreation and Parks Department, where she taught polymer clay classes to children and adults for several years.

While Debbie is multi-talented, her interests lie in creating ethnic-style polymer clay jewelry, dolls and home décor. Her work has appeared in numerous galleries and exhibitions across the country. Some of her work is published in *Polymer Clay: Creating Functional* and *Decorative Objects* by Jacqueline Gikow and *Polymer: The Chameleon Clay* by Victoria Hughes.

Debbie manages her own business, Debbie's Adornments, as an avenue to sell her work. She continues to teach at art conferences and other establishments. She served as president of the Columbus Polymer Clay Guild for several years and maintains membership with both the local and national guilds. Debbie also serves on the advisory board for *PolymerCAFÉ* magazine and is a member of the Ohio Designer Craftsmen.

08 07 06 05 04 5 4 3 2 1

Library of Congress Cataloging-in-Publication Data
Jackson, Debbie, 1950-
  Polymer clay jewelry / Debbie Jackson.--1st ed.
    p.cm.
  Includes index.
  ISBN 1-58180-513-6 (pbk. : alk. paper)
  1. Polymer clay craft. 2. Jewelry making. I. Title.

TT297.J33 2004
745.594'2--dc22
                          2003064996

Editor: Krista Hamilton
Designer: Joanna Detz
Layout Artist: Joni DeLuca
Production Coordinator: Sara Dumford
Photographer: Christine Polomsky, Tim Grondin and Al Parrish

Metric Conversion Chart

TO CONVERT	TO	MULTIPLY BY
Inches	Centimeters	2.54
Centimeters	Inches	0.4
Feet	Centimeters	30.5
Centimeters	Feet	0.03
Yards	Meters	0.9
Meters	Yards	1.1
Sq. Inches	Sq. Centimeters	6.45
Sq. Centimeters	Sq. Inches	0.16
Sq. Feet	Sq. Meters	0.09
Sq. Meters	Sq. Feet	10.8
Sq. Yards	Sq. Meters	0.8
Sq. Meters	Sq. Yards	1.2
Pounds	Kilograms	0.45
Kilograms	Pounds	2.2
Ounces	Grams	28.4
Grams	Ounces	0.035

DEDICATION

I dedicate this book to my beloved former polymer clay students from the Columbus Cultural Arts Center, who kept me informed of the latest tools and products and constantly challenged me to learn new techniques. But most importantly, you helped me learn more about myself, not only as a teacher, but also as a human being. Your loyalty and enthusiasm truly helped make it enjoyable for me to come to work each day.

I also dedicate this book to my much-admired Columbus Polymer Clay Guild, an outstanding (and growing) community of artisans and craftspersons committed to discovering numerous ways to work and play with polymer clay. Our friendship will be cherished forever!

ACKNOWLEDGMENTS

First and foremost, I'd like to thank my precious, loving God who blessed me with this book and gave me the strength and endurance to see it through.

"He who began a good work in you is faithful to complete it." Philippians 1:6

I honor my dear mother, Vernice Turner, who taught me to make an effort to finish things I start and strive to do my best. I acknowledge my gifted and talented sisters, Darla and Deedee, who touch my life in so many ways. I love you all so dearly! The precious women from my former Senior Citizen class, who have the ambition to learn, the patience to perform and the talent to create. I will always cherish the many interesting stories, moments of laughter and fabulous meals we shared. Thanks to Jennifer Johnson of the Columbus Cultural Arts Center, for all your support and praise throughout the years, and to Patty Harris for your support and encouragement. To Andrea Gilliland-Lewis of Prizm Artist's Supply Store, who generously provided the clay and some of the supplies for the projects in this book, and who has supported my teachings and students over the years.

Thank you, Sandy McKitrick, for helping my hands, and to Carol Shelton, for seeing in me what I couldn't see for myself and helping me start this journey.

I'd also like to acknowledge three of the many polymer clay artists who have influenced me in some way: Nan Roche, who wrote a book (*The New Clay*) that was ahead of its time, and one I still recommend to this day; Gwen Gibson, a technical genius, who continues to discover new materials to incorporate into our medium; and Tory Hughes, who unknowingly held my interest for years on-screen, as she taught me numerous ways to develop my ethnic style.

To the staff at F+W Publications, especially Tricia Waddell, who gave me encouragement, Krista Hamilton, who helped me become an author, and Christine Polomsky, who truly knows how to work a camera! Thanks to all of you!

Table of Contents

Introduction

Being a full-time polymer clay teacher has been so rewarding because I could teach, experiment and learn at the same time! If it wasn't for teaching, I wouldn't have experienced all the numerous ways of working with this exciting medium. The projects in this book are primarily the result of classes I have taught. Over the years, I have learned so much that I am bursting at the seams! Now I am able to share with you more technical skills, new discoveries of materials and supplies, and numerous tips and shortcuts on how to make your projects with ease. From years of experiments and attempts (some resulting in mishaps), I have found that there is always potential for a work in progress. After all, you are the boss...it's merely clay.

This book will help you intuitively start to mix colors more often, instead of using them right out of the package. The chapter on liquid polymer clay leads you into taking a deeper look at this unique material, discovering its multiple uses and effects. For those of you who love to make canes, I have designed a variety of new and fascinating patterns that will stimulate your creativity and imagination. I've also included projects that resemble some of the artistic styles of other cultures, including African, Asian, European and South American. I hope you enjoy the journey!

As I continue to experiment with this versatile material, I am constantly finding new things to do with it. I've also begun to take a look at things quite differently. I see patterns, colors, textures, images and even nature in a whole new way.

As a crafter, this book will introduce you to a fresh approach to working with polymer clay. I took pleasure in combining additional materials with polymer clay, resulting in several mixed media projects, as you will see in the Additives and Embellishments chapter and throughout the book. Whether you're a beginner or a "seasoned enthusiast," I hope you will find something that stimulates your creative process. Many of these techniques can be adapted to your very own style and will take off in a variety of directions.

In our crafting community, some of us find ourselves wishing we could turn this hobby into a business opportunity. This book will show you how to not only create the front of your piece, but also to finish the back. It will be just as interesting, and maybe even reversible. Even if you're not in the business, these practices will give your work a professional quality from start to finish.

GETTING STARTED

Tools and Supplies

One of the many benefits of working with polymer clay is the minimum amount of tools required. Though many of the tools and supplies needed for polymer clay are on the market, you'll find several practical things to use right in your home. Most of the tools and supplies listed here are used for the projects in this book.

Pasta Machines

Pasta machines are great for making flat, even sheets of clay in various thicknesses. Although it isn't necessary to purchase a pasta machine, it aids in conditioning clay, combining colors and creating patterned sheets, and is a must for making Skinner and rainbow blends (for instructions, see pages 16–19).

Pasta machines are easily found at cookware and department stores and can sometimes be found at thrift shops and yard sales. It is best to have a pasta machine that is dedicated to only polymer clay and not used for making pasta. Atlas is a widely known brand.

When it is time to clean your pasta machine, you can easily remove any oily film or bits of clay from the rollers with rubbing alcohol or baby wipes. Frequent use of your machine may cause clay to accumulate underneath and the blades to bulge. This bulge may distort your sheets of clay and may be a sign for you to take your machine apart to clean it thoroughly. The thought of this may sound scary, but asking a friend to help makes it much easier.

A HAND-CRANKED PASTA MACHINE SUCH AS THE ONE SHOWN HERE WILL HELP YOU CONDITION, BLEND AND ROLL YOUR CLAY INTO LONG, THIN SHEETS.

Motors

If you ever get tired of cranking your machine by hand, you may want to invest in a motorized machine. Although motors are a luxury, they make life easier when working with polymer clay. Using a motorized pasta machine enables you to hold the clay with both hands when making long sheets. Motors also shorten the process of making Skinner and rainbow blends, as the clay is run through 15 to 20 times without having to use the crank.

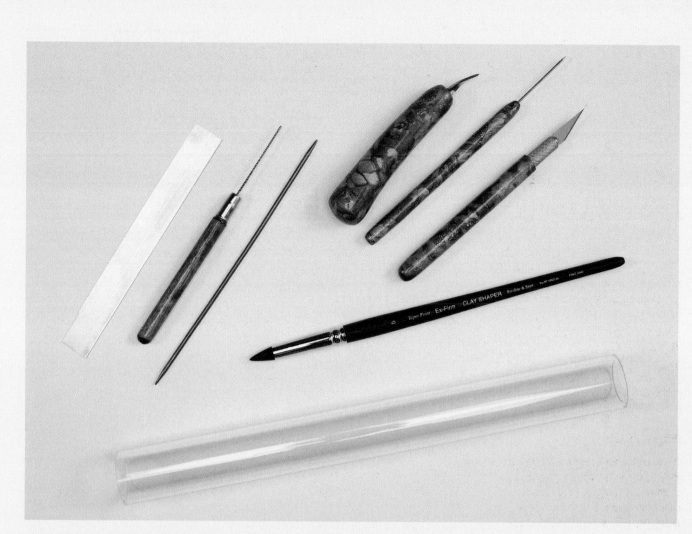

Make cutting and shaping clay easy with tools like the ones shown here: (clockwise from top) V-shaped fine line cutter; needle tool; X-Acto knife; clay shaper tool; acrylic roller; double-pointed knitting needle; hand drill; cutting blade.

Cutting Tools

Polymer clay cutting tools are used for cutting and slicing clay. I use four different types, each for a different function: the tissue blade, the Kato NuBlade, the Sculpey Super Slicer blade and the craft knife.

The blade I use most frequently is a tissue blade. It is not only good for opening packages of new clay, but it also works for slicing sheets, strips and canes. It can be bowed to cut an arc or curve, and it works well with the Mokume Gane technique (Mokume Gane Button, page 60). The tissue blade is extremely sharp and has a notch on the dull edge. Hold the notched edge with both hands and pull it taut as you cut.

I use the Kato NuBlade for its strength in cutting through thick chunks of clay. It is great for cutting slices off big canes and newly opened blocks of clay.

I keep a Sculpey Super Slicer blade on hand for cutting extremely thin slices of clay. This thin, flexible blade seems to maintain its sharpness longer than a tissue blade.

The craft knife is great for trimming clay out of tight, hard-to-reach spots. I use the X-Acto No. 11 Classic Fine Point blade for precision cutting, detailing and stripping clay. This knife is quite handy for trimming around the edge of a piece of clay while rotating it on paper.

Rolling Tools

I recommend using a clear, solid or hollow acrylic roller for compressing, smoothing and shaping polymer clay. The clay doesn't stick to the roller (as it does on a PVC pipe) and can easily be cleaned with rubbing alcohol or baby wipes. Other nonporous rollers I recommend include: acrylic brayers with handles, smooth drinking glasses, glass jars and bottles.

Piercing and Carving Tools

A needle tool is used for piercing holes into beads or sheets of clay. It can also texture a piece of raw clay for a perforated look. Other piercing tools include tapestry needles, double-pointed knitting needles, hatpins, toothpicks and bamboo skewers. For carving, I use a Speedball V-shaped Fine Line Cutter embedded and baked into a polymer clay handle as shown above. You can custom-design a variety of tools with handles to fit into your hand.

Add beauty and texture to your polymer clay with supplies such as the ones shown above: 400- and 600-grit wet/dry sandpaper; metallic leaf; Flecto Varathane Diamond Wood Finish in satin; Rub 'n Buff metallic rub-on paste; Pearl Ex powdered pigment; QuickTite superglue.

Sanding and Buffing Tools

A thin film forms on the surface of polymer clay after baking. To remove this film and even out the texture, I use 400-grit wet/dry sandpaper with water. Then, I use the finer 600-grit wet/dry sandpaper to remove the scratches made by the 400-grit paper. This will make the surface feel smooth. For a matte finish, I buff the sanded piece with a soft cloth. If I want a shiny surface, I polish the piece with a muslin buffing wheel on a Dremel tool, a Foredom bench lathe or a bench grinder.

Varnish

I enjoy the "natural" look of polymer clay, so I don't use varnish too often. Sometimes, it may cause the clay to look too much like plastic. Whenever I apply metallics such as gold leaf, Rub 'n Buff or powder, I apply a thin coat of varnish to protect and seal the surface.

Flecto Varathane Diamond Wood Finish in satin or gloss works well with polymer clay. Floor polish and varnishes made by polymer clay manufacturers are also practical choices.

Metallics

Metallic applications onto polymer clay create illuminating effects. They brighten and enhance the surface, making my pieces "pop." I use Rub 'n Buff, a wax-based metallic product, to highlight raised areas of my baked clay pieces. Metallic powders, like Jacquard's Pearl Ex powdered pigment, adhere easily to raw clay. The beautiful range of colors available can brighten any project. Metallic leaf comes in thin, fragile sheets in a variety of colors and patterns. It can be applied to raw or baked clay.

Adhesives

I use several types of glue for different purposes. Delta Sobo glue is a great tacky glue for adhering baked clay to raw clay. It also works well when adhering paper and other porous items to the clay. Superglue is great for bonding baked pieces together, metal jewelry findings to clay, gluing coiled ends onto leather cord, and many other uses in jewelry making. I prefer QuickTite (by Loctite) and Zap-A-Gap (by Pacer). These glues are very strong and bond instantly. I use both liquid and gel.

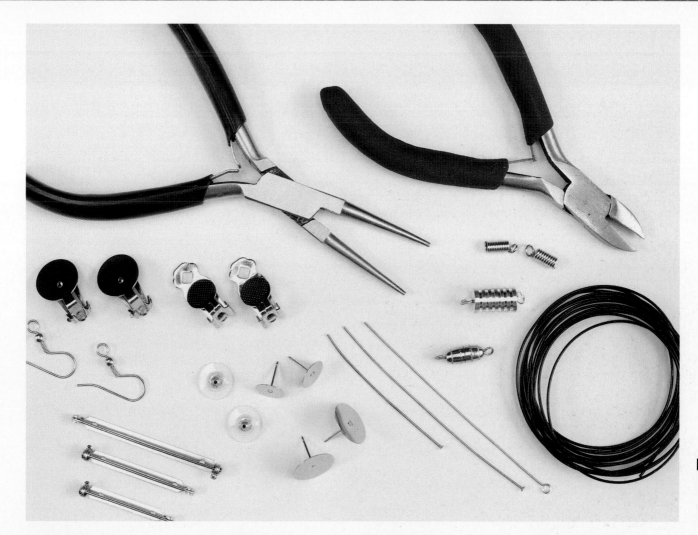

GOOD QUALITY TOOLS AND JEWELRY FINDINGS WILL MAKE ALL THE DIFFERENCE IN YOUR POLYMER CLAY CREATIONS. SHOWN ABOVE (CLOCKWISE FROM TOP) ARE: NEEDLE-NOSE PLIERS; WIRE CUTTERS; COIL ENDS; BARREL CLASPS; PLASTIC-COATED CRAFT WIRE; EYE PIN; HEAD PIN; FLAT PAD EARRING POSTS; EARRING NUTS; PIN BACKS; FRENCH HOOK EAR WIRES; CLIP BACKS.

Jewelry Tools

Needle-nose pliers, also called round-nose pliers, are good for bending, curving and looping wire into all shapes and sizes. Wire cutters, or side cutters, are used for cutting wire clean and true. Crimping pliers are used for making crimp beads and tubes into clean, round forms instead of squashing them flat.

Jewelry Findings

Whether you market your jewelry or not, it is best to use good-quality findings on your work. After putting all that labor of love into your projects, it's certainly worth a few extra dollars to spend on superior findings. Pin backs should have secure, reliable clasps, and no-snag, sharply pointed stems. Flat pad earring posts should be of superior quality with reinforced assembly so the post won't break off.

If you're not ready to afford sterling earring wires or trained to make them, buying 22-gauge surgical stainless steel earring wires may be the next best thing. It is better than the less-expensive plated brass wires, which have a tendency to flake off when the earring wire loop is bent.

There are so many types of commercial necklace clasps to choose from: barrel, toggle, hook, spring ring and even magnetic clasps. My decision on which clasp to use depends on the design and weight of the necklace I've made. For those who are innovative, you can design your own creative clasp!

Discovering Polymer Clay

THERE ARE SEVERAL VARIETIES OF POLYMER CLAY, EACH WITH SPECIFIC CHARACTERISTICS. SHOWN HERE ARE FIMO CLASSIC POLYMER CLAY, FIMO SOFT POLYMER CLAY, KATO LIQUID POLYCLAY (TM) CLEAR MEDIUM (LEFT) AND PREMO POLYMER CLAY (BELOW).

Polymer clay is a modeling medium composed of polyvinyl chloride (PVC), pigment and plasticizer. It comes in an array of beautiful colors and is easily available at your local craft store or through the Internet. This medium is one of the most versatile I've ever seen! It can be carved, textured, painted, buffed, stamped and drilled. I love the way it can simulate bone, ivory, wood, leather, fabric, metal and semiprecious stones. Polymer clay is moldable and won't dry out when stored at room temperature, and it hardens when baked in a regular, convection or toaster oven.

I use different brands of polymer clay for different reasons, and here is why: When I first began my "clay journey," I bought a soft, inexpensive clay that was easy to condition. I found out the hard way that this clay becomes brittle when baked, and the jewelry I made was breaking easily.

As I became more involved in the craft, I took a flower cane class at a local bead store. The teacher used Fimo Classic. From that point on, I have used Fimo Classic for its durability and workability when making canes (you will learn more about canes in Chapter 5). My hands get warm when working with clay, and canes made with some brands of clay have actually compressed and smeared when I cut them because they were too soft. Nothing is more frustrating than building a beautiful cane, only to find that it collapses after the first cut. If you like using softer clay and this happens to you, let it sit for a while or put it in the refrigerator to cool. Although most of the cane projects in this book use Fimo Classic brand polymer clay, feel free to use the clay that works best for you.

I use Premo brand polymer clay for the remaining projects in this book. Premo is flexible and durable when baked, and it conditions easily right out of the package. It is also soft enough for texturing and embedding. I especially love Premo's mica-based pearlescents. They add a whole new dimension to my pieces.

Several other brands of polymer clay, such as Kato Polyclay, are on the market, all of which have their advantages and disadvantages. At the time of this writing, I've had very little experience with Kato Polyclay. So far, I have found that it is easy to condition, canes well and remains flexible after baking. Experiment with all of them, or mix them together, until you find your perfect clay combination.

Conditioning Polymer Clay

In order to begin working with polymer clay, you must first condition it. This will soften the clay and improve its workability. One way to condition polymer clay is to work it with your hands. Roll a snake, fold it in half and twist it. Repeat this process until the clay is pliable and doesn't crack when folded.

Another way to condition polymer clay is by running it through a pasta machine. These machines are available in cook stores, on many cooking and craft supply web sites, and even at some flea markets and garage sales. Pasta machines have adjustable settings that make the sheets of clay come out in different thicknesses. In this book, I will refer to the settings on the Atlas brand pasta machine. The #1 setting is the thickest, #2 to #5 are medium, and #6 and #7 are thin. I don't condition all brands of clay the same way, as some are softer than others and may not need as much attention. Follow the steps below to condition your clay.

1. Cut Clay
Cut thin slices off a block of polymer clay with a tissue blade and overlap them slightly.

2. Form Sheet
Arrange the slices back together to form one sheet.

Conditioning Polymer Clay

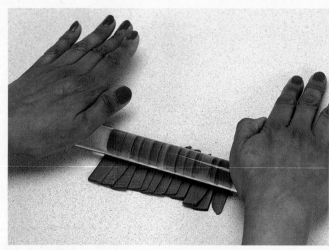

3. Compress to Flatten
Firmly compress the sheet of clay with an acrylic roller to flatten it.

4. Remove Excess Clay
Scrape the sheet off the work surface with a table knife.

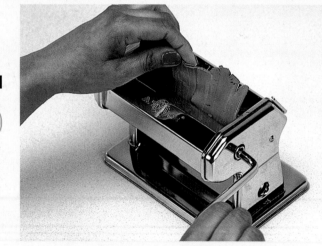

5. Run Sheet Through Pasta Machine
Run the sheet through the pasta machine on the #1 setting.

6. Repeat
Fold the flat sheet in half and reinsert it into the pasta machine fold-side first. Repeat this 12 to 15 times or until the consistency is soft and workable.

Mixing Colors

Although many beautiful colors of polymer clay are on the market, I enjoy mixing my own to get the results I need. After a brief study of color theory, I am now able to mix colors to match fabrics and home interiors.

In working with polymer clay, I have found that some colors darken after baking. Adding a portion of white, yellow, ecru, fluorescent or a pastel of the original color makes it lighter and brighter.

Colors can be mixed by rolling and twisting by hand, or they can be run through a pasta machine until thoroughly blended, as shown below.

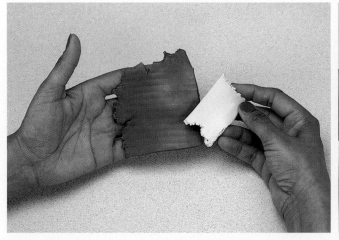

1. Overlap Clay
Overlap two sheets of conditioned polymer clay in contrasting colors. Here I'm mixing a small amount of white with green to create a lighter shade of green.

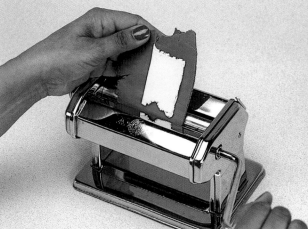

2. Run Sheet Through Pasta Machine
Run the sheet through the pasta machine on the #1 setting. To speed up the mixing process, run the sheet through the machine on sequential settings: #1, #2, #3 and #4.

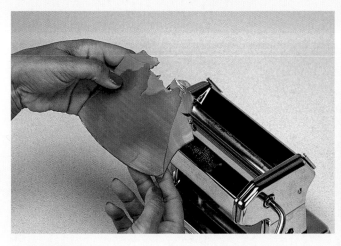

3. Repeat
Fold and repeat. The clay will develop a marbled appearance as the colors begin to mix.

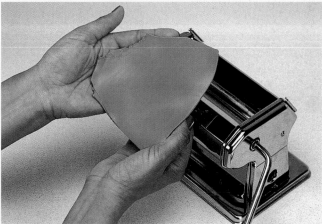

4. Observe Final Color
Continue to fold and run the clay through the pasta machine until the colors are evenly mixed. Add more white to achieve an even lighter shade.

Making a Skinner Blend

I used to hand-mix proportions of contrasting clays from dark to light to create more depth in my canes. This procedure took up a lot of studio time, and the proportions weren't always easy to figure out.

Then I heard about the Skinner blend, developed by Judith Skinner. It is a quick and easy way of combining two colors to get a beautiful, graduated sheet of clay with an airbrushed effect.

Once the sheet has been made, it can be manipulated in a variety of ways. You can use a portion of the sheet for a landscape scene, like a sunset. It makes a great background on which to scatter cane slices or strips of clay. You can even fold it into accordion pleats, roll it into a bull's-eye cane or cut it into strips and stack them. The possibilities are endless.

Thank you, Judith Skinner!

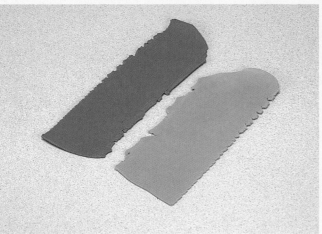

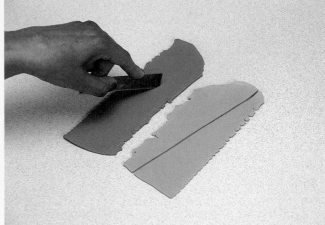

1. Condition Clay
Condition two pieces of clay in contrasting colors and run each piece through the pasta machine on the #1 setting.

2. Cut Into Triangles
Use your tissue blade to cut each piece diagonally, making elongated triangles.

3. Form Rectangle
Using one triangle of each color, place the diagonal ends of the clay together, staggering the triangles and overlapping them slightly to form a rectangle.

Tip

To double the amount of clay in your Skinner blend, flip the remaining triangle of the same color onto itself. Repeat with the other color.

4. Trim Ends and Smooth
Trim off the ends with a tissue blade and smooth the seam with an acrylic roller.

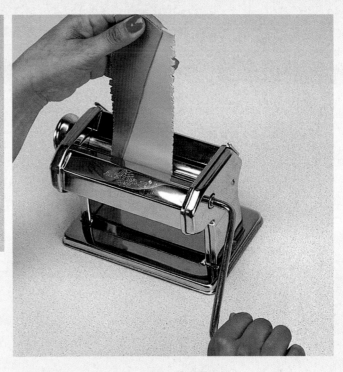

5. Run Sheet Through Pasta Machine
Run the two-toned rectangular sheet through the pasta machine on the #3 setting.

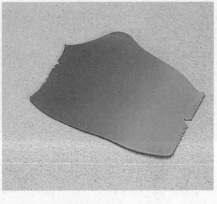

8. Observe End Result
The end result will look airbrushed with the colors blending smoothly into each other.

7. Continue Until Streaks Disappear
Continue this process until there are no longer any streaks.

6. Fold and Repeat
Fold the piece in half and run it through again, fold-side first.

Making a Rainbow Blend

The rainbow blend is a variation of the Skinner blend. You can use infinite color combinations to create beautiful effects such as a rainbow jelly roll or bull's-eye and a variety of textile patterns.

To prepare for this blend, condition five pieces of polymer clay in contrasting colors and run each through the pasta machine on the #3 setting. As you condition, add ⅛ block of white clay to each color. I used the following colors to achieve the rainbow blend shown below: cobalt blue, fuchsia, orange, yellow and turquoise.

1. Trim Sheets
Using a craft knife, trim each prepared clay sheet to measure 2½" x 7" (6cm x 18cm).

18

2. Make Triangles
Cut each sheet in half diagonally, making elongated triangles.

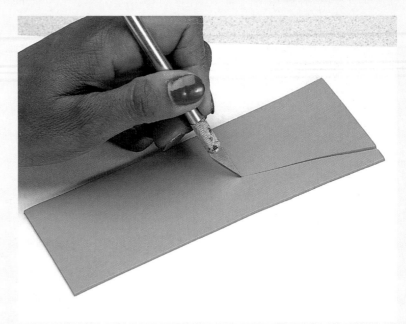

3. Invert Triangles

Place the triangles together, inverting every other triangle and overlapping them slightly.

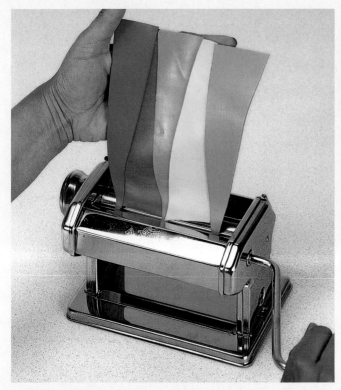

4. Run Through Pasta Machine

Run the sheet through the pasta machine on the #3 setting. Repeat this process 12 to 15 times, folding top to bottom after each pass and feeding the clay into the machine fold-side first.

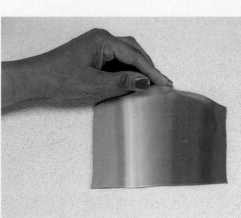

5. Repeat Until Blended

Repeat until the sheet has an airbrushed appearance and colors are well-blended.

Tip

When making any sort of blend, always put the folded side of the sheet into the machine first, making sure all the colors enter the machine vertically.

Laminating

Thin, fragile or sheer materials can be made stronger and more durable by coating them with liquid polymer clay. This process, known as laminating, works great on metallic leaf, magazine and catalog pictures, dried leaves, lace, thin fabrics and decorative papers, which can be coated on one or both sides. Once baked, laminated clay pieces can be precisely cut with scissors and bent into a variety of shapes without worry of tearing.

Although several brands of liquid polymer clay are on the market, I prefer Translucent Liquid Sculpey (TLS) for laminating purposes. It is milky in consistency and dries clear. I have used TLS for the majority of the liquid polymer clay projects in this book. You will learn more about liquid polymer clay in Chapter 4.

Laminated items have many uses. For instance, you can make collage jewelry by gluing laminated shapes onto baked clay, glass or wood; cut and weave strips of laminated material to create one-of-a-kind art; or even sew pieces together to add texture to your work. My imagination is flying just thinking about it!

1. Apply Liquid Polymer Clay
Apply a medium coat of Translucent Liquid Sculpey (TLS) to a sheet of glass. (I used glass from a picture frame.)

2. Spread Liquid Polymer Clay
Use a soft, flat paintbrush to spread the TLS in cross-hatch directions to form an even coat.

3. Apply Metallic Leaf

Lift a sheet of metallic leaf delicately and place it on the coated glass. Remove the excess metallic leaf with a craft knife. Bake for 15 minutes at 300° F (150° C). Allow to cool.

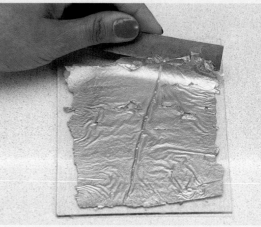

4. Coat Other Side

Using a tissue blade, carefully peel the metallic leaf off the glass and turn it over to the untreated side. Coat this side with TLS.

5. Smooth Liquid Polymer Clay

Smooth the TLS to medium thickness with a soft, flat paintbrush. Bake for 15 minutes at 300° F (150° C). Allow to cool.

6. Remove Metallic Leaf

Carefully remove the baked sheet of laminated metallic leaf from the glass with a tissue blade. Cut the sheet into interesting shapes and adhere them to jewelry projects or store them until you are ready to use them.

Tip

Whenever you laminate fabrics, always make test samples, as some fabrics will darken when coated with liquid polymer clay.

Making a Push Mold

Polymer clay is a wonderful medium to use for making molds. Molds are great for reproducing detailed items to use in your work. Some molds can even be used for making textures or backgrounds. My favorite objects to use for making push molds are African brass masks, wooden Balinese stamps, vintage buttons, costume jewelry and rubber stamps. The following steps demonstrate how to make a push mold.

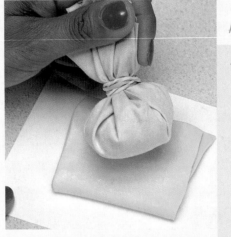

Tip

To make your own pouncer, cut out two 5" (13cm) square pieces of lightweight cotton fabric. Add a few tablespoons of baby powder, talcum powder or cornstarch to the center of the fabric. Bring all four corners together and wrap with a rubber band or tie with a string to close. I thank Gwen Gibson for sharing this helpful tip with me!

1. Fold Clay
Condition one block of clay and run it through the pasta machine on the #1 setting. Fold the sheet in half to double it, then fold it again to quadruple the thickness. Flatten slightly with an acrylic roller.

2. Powder Clay
Lightly tamp powder on the clay with a powder pouncer (instructions at right) to prevent it from sticking to your object. Be sure to wipe off any excess powder. Otherwise, the residue will be extremely difficult to remove after baking.

3. Impress Object
Center the wooden stamp or selected object on the raw clay and press firmly, making sure the desired pattern is impressed. With your fingers, firmly push raw clay against the wooden stamp.

4. Trim Excess Clay
Gently lift the object to reveal the impressed image. Trim excess clay with a round cookie cutter or tissue blade. Bake for one hour at 275° F (135° C). Allow to cool.

To use this as a mold, roll a small ball of conditioned clay until smooth. Lightly tamp it with powder and press the clay firmly into the mold. Remove the clay and trim off the excess with a craft knife. Smooth the edges. Bake at 275° F (135° C) for 30 minutes. (For more about making and using molds, see page 62.)

Baking

Because polymer clay does not air-dry, it must be "cured," or baked in a toaster oven or convection oven, to be hardened. The oven should be used for the sole purpose of baking polymer clay, not for preparing food. Bake the clay at a temperature range between 265°–275° F (130°–135° C), depending on the manufacturer's suggestions on the package of the brand you are using.

I do not recommend using a regular kitchen oven to bake your clay since it is used to prepare food. If you must, be sure to wipe off any residue thoroughly before using it for food. When using a toaster oven, make sure you cover your clay with a "tent" of aluminum foil or a pie pan. Quite often, the elements turn red during baking, therefore scorching the clay and causing toxic fumes. Always bake in a well-ventilated room.

I cannot stress enough the importance of using an oven thermometer. Never trust the accuracy of the numbers on the knobs outside your oven. A good thermometer will tell me the truth about what is happening on the inside. Leave it in the oven the entire time you're baking to make sure it is maintaining the desired temperature.

To cure a piece, bake it for a minimum of 30 minutes. If you are baking the same piece multiple times, bake it in 15–20 minute intervals. This will prepare the piece for the next procedure. An underbaked piece of clay will break more easily. Remember this rule: "The longer, the stronger," as long as the oven is at the proper temperature.

Place the pieces to be baked on heavy paper or mat board. I like to place my pieces on smooth, heavy mat board for baking. It doesn't warp and maintains its shape, unlike weaker paper. Other baking sheet liners include manila folders, strong cardboard, parchment and watercolor papers.

When baking beads or dimensional pieces, place them on polyester batting with mat board underneath. This cushions the piece so it will maintain its shape. A curved piece may flatten or a bead may end up with a flat spot without the batting for support.

Storing

After opening a pack of polymer clay, store the unused portion in a plastic sandwich bag or surround it with plastic wrap. Do not store clay in wax paper, parchment paper or typing paper, as the oil will be absorbed from the clay. This process, called "leaching," can be done when your clay is too oily and you want to remove some of the oil.

I keep my clay in the drawers of a portable plastic storage unit on wheels, sorted by brand and color. To conserve space (and save time), flatten the clay with a roller or pasta machine. Lay the sheets into sandwich bags or cover in plastic wrap and stack them into a polystyrene storage box.

Make sure to keep your clay away from a sunny window. Otherwise, it may dry out. Do not leave it in your car in the hot summer or cold winter. These are just a few ways to help extend the shelf life of your clay.

Additives and Embellishments

As a collector of "stuff" over the years, I have gathered an interesting array of baubles, beads, costume jewelry, shells, bones, foreign coins, charms and many other fascinating trinkets. They are stored in their own special space, just waiting to be used at the right moment. In this section, there are three wonderful projects for you to create using embellishments.

My love of African beads inspires me to use them in my jewelry compositions and as dangling elements attached to my pendants. Another way to use them is to attach them to the top surface of the clay and fill the hole with raffia or Mizuhiki cord. The African Brass Brooch project (page 26) demonstrates how a flat bead is embedded into a piece of clay to embellish it.

My interest in making hatpins derived from a month-long, community wide celebration of making and wearing hats, entitled, "Hey, Columbus, What's on Your Head?" I began to make a collection of one-of-a-kind hatpins to sell during the celebration. I even taught a class on how to make them. The experience made me enjoy pin-making even more. It is a great way to use some of the trinkets I've saved over the years, like the feathers and shells in the Feathered Hatpin project (page 32).

Movable jewelry pieces really intrigue me, so I try to incorporate them into my art on occasion. After learning a variety of ways to make hinges, I found that the coil hinge is one of my favorites. The Hinged Dragonfly Pendant (page 36) shows an alternate way to add rubber stamped clay elements to any composition.

African Brass Brooch

This project shows how to embellish a textured piece of clay using a flat brass bead. Filling the hole with decorative Japanese paper cord, also called Mizuhiki cord, introduces an added dimension.

MATERIALS

- ½ block of turquoise polymer clay (Premo)
- ⅛ block of black polymer clay (Premo)
- translucent liquid polymer clay (Translucent Liquid Sculpey [TLS])
- gold metallic leaf
- African brass embellishment
- one ¼" (6mm) pin back
- small cane slices
- Mizuhiki cord

- 4" x 8" (10cm x 20cm) cardstock
- dimensional wallpaper or texture sheet
- wire mesh screen
- sanding screen
- 1" x 1½" (2.5cm x 3.8cm) oval cutter
- craft knife
- tissue blade
- pasta machine
- pouncer (for instructions, see page 22)

- superglue
- acrylic roller
- acrylic tile
- clay shaper tool
- polyester batting
- varnish
- pattern (page 123)

1. Cut Out Template

Condition ½ block of turquoise clay and run it through the pasta machine on the #2 setting. Cut the clay sheet in half and set one half aside. Cut out the pattern provided on page 123 and place it on the prepared clay sheet. Trim around the edges with a craft knife.

2. Powder Clay

Lightly powder the clay with a pouncer (for instructions, see page 22), wiping away any excess. When you press a texturing agent into the clay, the powder will prevent it from sticking.

Tip

Use cardstock or scrap paper as a turntable to rotate the piece with ease.

3. Texture Clay
Press dimensional wallpaper or the material of your choice into the clay and roll with an acrylic roller.

4. Prepare Black Clay
Condition ⅛ block of black clay and run it through the pasta machine on the #5 setting. Lightly powder the clay with a pouncer and wipe away the excess. Place wire mesh on top of the clay and impress the pattern with an acrylic roller.

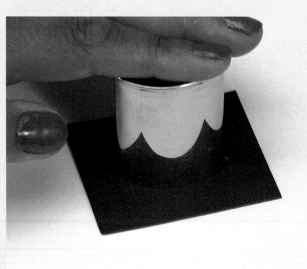

5. Cut Out Oval
Use a 1" x 1½" (2.5cm x 3.8cm) oval cutter to cut an oval from the black clay. Set the excess clay aside for later use.

6. Add Oval
Center the black oval onto the turquoise base. Gently press with your fingers to attach the pieces together.

Tip

You can use lace, linen, screen, mesh or any other dimensional surface to texture your clay.

7. Roll Snake in Gold Leaf

Roll the excess black clay from step 5 into a snake measuring approximately ⅛" x 2" (3mm x 5cm). Roll the snake over gold metallic leaf until it is covered.

8. Crackle Gold Leaf

Using both hands, roll and stretch the snake to 4" (10cm) or the perimeter of the black oval. This will cause the gold leaf to crackle. Place an acrylic tile on top of the snake and roll it back and forth to even out the snake and remove finger grooves.

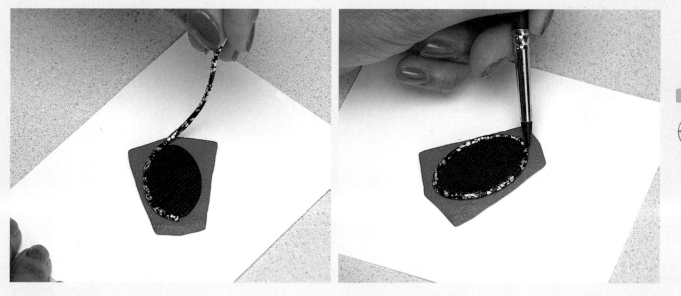

9. Outline Oval

Outline the black oval with the snake and trim off any excess. Gently press with your fingers to attach the pieces together.

10. Clean Up Edges

Clean up the edges of the snake piece and tap down the seam with a clay shaper tool.

11. Apply Glue to Embellishment
Add a few drops of superglue to the back of an African brass embellishment or the decoration of your choice.

12. Adhere Embellishment
Center the embellishment in the middle of the black oval and press down for about 20 seconds. Bake for 20 minutes at 275° F (135° C). Allow to cool.

13. Prepare Clay for Pin Back
To make the back of your pin, run the remaining turquoise clay from step 1 through the pasta machine on the #4 setting. Texture the sheet with a sanding screen or the material of your choice. Trace the provided pattern onto the clay and trim away excess with a craft knife.

14. Apply TLS
Apply a thin coat of TLS onto the back of the baked piece.

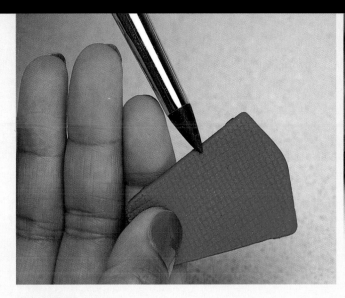

15. Add Raw Clay

Place the raw piece of turquoise clay on top of the TLS, textured-side out. Smooth the edges with a clay shaper tool to remove the seam.

16. Adhere Pin Back

Superglue the pin back to the upper third of the raw clay and press for 20 seconds.

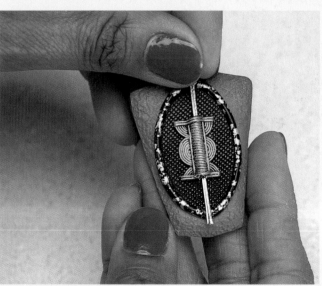

17. Add Cane Slices

Cut several thin slices from a cane or scrap piece of clay with a tissue blade. Spread a thin coat of TLS on the back of the slices and compress each one over the pin back to conceal it. Bake the piece facedown on polyester batting for 25 minutes at 275° F (135° C). When cool, brush a thin coat of clear varnish over the gold leaf snake. This will prevent the leafing from flecking off.

18. Add Cord

Cut four or five strands of Mizuhiki cord to 2" (5cm) or desired length. Insert the strands through the hole in the African brass embellishment. Apply a few drops of superglue into the hole to secure the cord.

Feathered Hatpin

Even if you're not a hat-wearer, you'll still have plenty of places to display this fancy piece. Use it to decorate the lapel of your jacket or coat, or to secure a scarf. You can even cluster several hatpins on a garment to make a fashion statement!

MATERIALS

- ½ block of burnt umber polymer clay (Premo)
- liquid polymer clay (Translucent Liquid Sculpey [TLS])
- 6" (15cm) hatpin with clutch
- two flat cowrie shells
- feathers
- ostrich shell beads
- African batik bone bead
- small beige bone beads
- metal crimp bead
- onion bag or texture sheet
- 1¼" x 2" (3.2cm x 5.1cm) teardrop-shaped cutter
- tissue blade
- pasta machine
- acrylic roller
- needle-nose pliers
- crimping pliers
- clay shaper tool
- needle tool
- scissors
- superglue gel

1. Texture Clay

Condition ½ block of burnt umber clay and run it through the pasta machine on the #2 setting. Texture the prepared clay by placing a mesh onion bag over the clay sheet. Roll an acrylic roller across the mesh to partially embed it into the clay. Carefully peel off the mesh.

2. Cut Out Teardrops

Use a teardrop-shaped cutter to cut out two teardrops. Cut about ½" (1cm) off the bottom of each teardrop with a tissue blade and set one teardrop aside for later use.

3. Add Crimped Hatpin

Crimp the blunt end of a 6" (15cm) hatpin about ½" (1cm) by zigzagging the wire back and forth with needle-nose pliers. Embed the crimped end into the raw clay of one teardrop and secure with superglue gel.

4. Adhere Cowrie Shell

Flip the piece over. Apply superglue gel to the flat side of the cowrie shell and press it firmly into the raw clay.

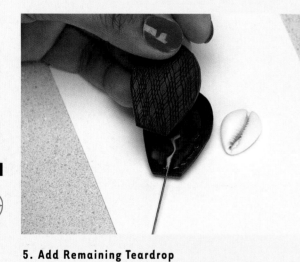

5. Add Remaining Teardrop

Spread TLS on the back of the first teardrop, then place the remaining teardrop on top, encasing the hatpin.

6. Adhere Remaining Cowrie Shell

Glue a cowrie shell to the second teardrop, pressing from both sides to secure. Blend the seam on the outer edge with a clay shaper tool or by stroking it with your thumb.

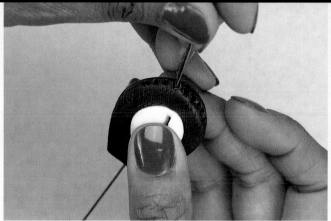

7. Drill Holes

Use a needle tool to make nine holes around the perimeter of the clay, spacing the holes about $1/8$" (3mm) apart. Bake for 25 minutes at 275° F (135° C). Allow to cool.

8. Prepare Feathers

Trim the down from several feathers with scissors.

9. Insert Feathers

Apply superglue gel sparingly to the tips of the feathers and insert them into the holes.

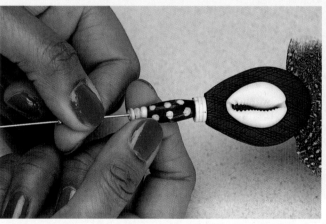

10. Add Embellishments

Slide the ostrich shell beads up the hatpin and secure them in place. Repeat with the African batik bone bead and any other small beads you desire. Finish with a metal crimp bead and squeeze it flat to secure with crimping pliers.

Tip

If a bead hole is too large, fill it with raw clay, then slide the bead up the hatpin and glue in place. There is no need to bake this again.

Hinged Dragonfly Pendant

Create a whole new dimension with your deeply cut rubber stamps by carving them out to create a lace-like texture. This project also invites you to use those charms or single earrings you've been saving.

MATERIALS

- 1 block of black polymer clay (Premo)
- ½ block of cadmium red polymer clay (Premo)
- liquid polymer clay (Translucent Liquid Sculpey [TLS])
- ginkgo leaf stamp (available from Creative Claystamps)
- assorted beads
- necklace cord
- two coil ends with loops
- necklace barrel clasp
- small leaf cane (optional)
- wire mesh screen or texture sheets

- 2' (61cm) of 22-gauge black craft wire
- cardstock
- craft knife
- tissue blade
- 1³/₄" x 2¹/₄" (4.5cm x 5.7cm) oval cutter (medium)
- 2¹/₄" x 2⁷/₈" (5.7cm x 7.3cm) oval cutter (large)
- wire cutters
- scissors
- baby powder and pouncer
- clay shaper tool
- stiff paintbrush
- pasta machine

- acrylic roller
- double-pointed knitting needle
- needle tool
- needle-nose pliers
- wire cutters
- superglue
- back pattern (page 122)
- pad pattern (page 122)

1. Impress Image Into Clay
Condition 1 block of black clay on the #3 setting. Cut the clay sheet to the size of the ginkgo leaf stamp or the rubber stamp of your choice. Lightly powder one side of the clay and place it on top of the stamp. Powder the top of the clay and "walk" your fingers across the surface to impress the image. Continue to press the clay into the stamp until the image appears.

2. Remove Clay From Stamp
Peel the clay from the stamp carefully by rolling the outer edges away from the stamp. Place the textured clay on cardstock or scrap paper.

3. Cut Oval

Use a medium oval cutter to cut out an oval shape from the stamped clay. Set aside the remaining clay for use in step 6.

4. Cut Between Patterns

Gently cut out pieces of clay from between the stamped patterns with a sharp craft knife. Bake for 20 minutes at 275° F (135° C). Allow to cool.

5. Adhere Red Oval

Condition ½ block of cadmium red clay on the #3 setting. Texture the red sheet of clay with wire mesh or the texture sheet of your choice. Cut out a medium oval from the red clay. Apply a thin coat of TLS to the back of the baked black oval. Place it on top of the medium red oval, pressing firmly. Bake for 15 minutes at 275° F (135° C). Allow to cool.

6. Make Frame

To make the frame, run the remaining black clay from step 3 through the pasta machine on the #1 setting. Cut the sheet in half and run one half through on the #4 setting. Stack one black sheet on top of the other and place the baked oval on top of the layered raw pieces. Trim the raw clay around the outer edge of the baked oval with a craft knife.

7. Remove Center

Remove the oval cut-out from the raw clay and set it aside. Place the baked oval in the hole so that it is surrounded by the raw clay.

8. Cut Out Frame

Press the raw clay against the baked oval to seal the seam. Center a large oval cutter over the entire piece and press down to cut out the frame.

9. Texture Frame

Texture the frame with sandpaper, tapering the edges as you go. This helps to remove fingerprints and gives it a nice finish. Bake for 20 minutes at 275° F (135° C). Allow to cool.

10. Add Canes

Run the remainder of the black clay from step 7 through on the #1 setting. Slice paper-thin leaf canes or other cane patterns and place them on the sheet of clay in a random pattern. Roll with an acrylic roller to adhere the cane slices and texture with mesh screen.

Tip

Scattering cane slices onto a clay sheet is a good way to use up your end pieces of old canes. This also makes the back of your pendant look as interesting as the front, sometimes making it reversible!

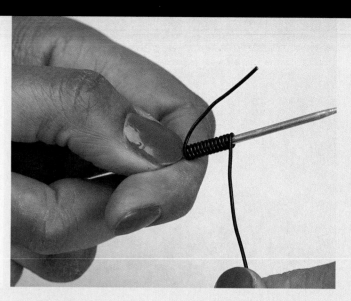

11. Make Pendant Back
Cut out the pattern on page 122 for the back of the pendant. Place the pattern on the clay sheet from step 10 and cut out the shape with a craft knife. Set the piece aside for use in step 15.

12. Make Coil for Hinge
To make the hinge, use wire cutters to cut a 14" (36cm) piece of 22-gauge wire. Wrap it in a tight coil around a knitting needle, leaving a tail approximately 2" (5cm) long. The coil should be no wider than the pendant's top.

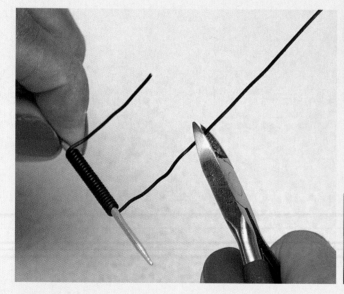

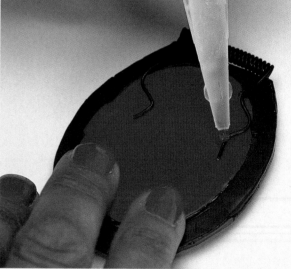

13. Crimp Legs
Cut another 2" (5cm) leg with wire cutters. Crimp both legs with needle-nose pliers by bending them back and forth. Slide the coil off the knitting needle.

14. Adhere Legs
Place the pendant facedown and position the coil on the upper edge of the piece with the legs hanging down. Superglue the legs in place and hold for 20 seconds, pressing with a needle tool.

Tip

Always crimp wire when embedding it into clay. This gives it a better grasp and prevents it from slipping out when worn.

15. Adhere Pendant Back

Use a stiff paintbrush to spread a thin coat of TLS onto the back piece from step 11. Adhere the piece to the baked oval to conceal the hinge and smooth the seams with a clay shaper tool or your thumb. Bake for 25 minutes at 275° F (135° C). Allow to cool. Cut 8" (20cm) of 22-gauge wire and string it through the coil. Bend the wire at 45° angles on both ends.

16. Make Pad

To make the pad above the hinge, run a sheet of black clay through the pasta machine on the #1 setting. Fold the sheet in half to double the thickness and measure about 1" x 3" (3cm x 8cm). Apply leaf cane slices and texture with mesh screen as you did with the back piece in step 10. Cut out the pad pattern provided on page 122, center it over the clay and cut out the shape with a craft knife.

17. Drill Holes

Position the pad over the bent wire from step 15 and mark the entry points with a needle tool. Use the needle tool to drill holes all the way through the top section at the markings.

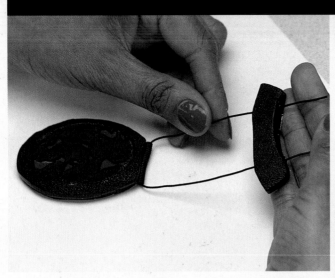

18. String Wires

String the wires through the holes and slide the pad all the way down to the hinge of the pendant. Tidy up the edges and add texture with more sandpaper if desired. Bake for 30 minutes at 275° F (135° C). Allow to cool.

19. Add Beads

String decorative beads onto the wires on one side of the pendant and use needle-nose pliers to roll the wires forward, creating coils.

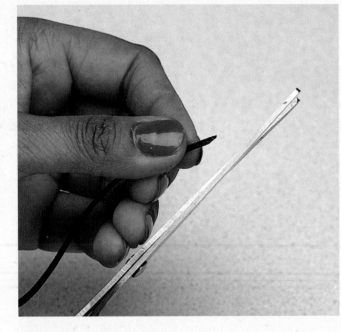

21. Thread Cord

Thread the cord through one set of coils. Add beads of your choice and continue to thread the cord through the second set of coils. Center the pendant on the cord.

20. Prepare Cord

Measure the length of necklace cord that you desire for the pendant. Cut the ends of the cord at an angle with craft scissors and add a drop of superglue so the ends won't unravel.

22. Secure Cord

Trim the cord slightly as you push it all the way into the coil. Add a drop of superglue to the top of the coil. Allow the glue to dry. Repeat on the other side.

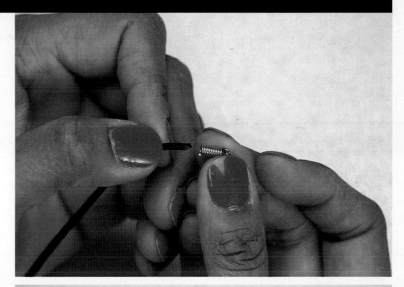

23. Finish Coil

Using the flat edge of your needle-nose pliers, crimp the last loop of the end coil to secure it. Round off the wire by rotating the coil. This will prevent it from scratching your neck.

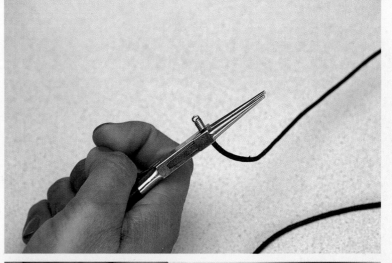

24. Add Barrel Clasp

Open the loop of a barrel clasp with needle-nose pliers. Hook the clasp onto the end coil and close the loop with the pliers.

Additives and Embellishments Gallery

Kimono Necklace

I DESIGNED A TEMPLATE TO CREATE THIS NECKLACE, WHICH IS REVERSIBLE. THE RUBBER STAMPED CLAY WAS BAKED, THEN HIGHLIGHTED WITH GOLD RUB 'N BUFF AND EMBELLISHED WITH AN ORIENTAL CHARM. THE OPPOSITE SIDE IS BLACK TEXTURED CLAY WITH A CHINESE COIN. I ATTACHED BUNA CORD TO AN FERN STEM TO ADD AN EXOTIC FLAIR.

Japanese Pouch Earrings

I STITCHED VINTAGE JAPANESE OBI FABRIC AND STUFFED IT WITH BATTING TO CREATE THESE CHARMING, PURSE-LIKE EARRINGS. NOTICE HOW THE BRIGHT RED, SCREEN-TEXTURED POLYMER CLAY FLAPS, COMPLETE WITH JET RHINESTONES, REALLY POP.

Mudcloth Brooch

I made this brooch with an arched, prebaked mudcloth cane slice and embellished it with a cowrie shell and ostrich shell beads embedded into unbaked, textured clay. After baking, I glued raffia into the opening and used cane slices to cover the pin back.

Cowrie Shell Brooch

For this sparkly piece, I embedded a cowrie shell into a crackled silver leaf clay sheet and embellished it with leaf cane slices for added dimension.

African Hut Brooch

Here, I mixed red clay from Georgia into translucent polymer clay, resulting in a granular texture for the walls and outer edges of this brooch. The Georgia pine needles give the appearance of a thatched roof. The plants are made from leftover leaf canes, and the flower pot is a small bamboo bead.

Textures

I rarely create a piece of polymer clay jewelry that doesn't have some kind of texture. Polymer clay takes on the feel of what it is surrounded by, baked on or pressed into. I have a great collection of texture sheets, materials and tools so I can continue to add visual and tactile quality to my work. The projects in this section represent just a few of the many ways texture can be achieved.

I appreciate the beauty and simplicity of Japanese art. The fan is one of my favorite patterns, representing the unfolding of good fortune. For the Oriental Fan Hatpin (page 48), I used a commercially made texture sheet. It has an appropriate pattern for this theme: repeating waves, which are often seen on silk kimonos.

Molas are colorful, appliquéd panels, hand-stitched by the Cuna women in Panama. They portray both aquatic and land-dwelling animals. I designed the Mola Pendant (page 52) with a simple bird pattern, one of the most common figures used in mola designs. For me, carving is a very relaxing way to create texture.

My friend Benja, who makes fabulous jackets and coats, asked me to design matching buttons for her creations. Making buttons is not only fun, but it is also a challenge to make sure the buttons match the fabric. Mokume Gane is a Japanese metalworking technique in which different colors of metal are layered, manipulated, then cut away to reveal various patterns. The Mokume Gane Button (page 60) introduces lots of colors and patterns into an otherwise plain background.

Oriental Fan Hatpin

You can make this reversible hatpin in just about any texture. This project gives you an opportunity to select a piece from your textured materials collection and peruse your stash of origami or handmade papers.

MATERIALS

- 1 block of black polymer clay (Premo)
- liquid polymer clay (Translucent Liquid Sculpey [TLS])
- 6" (15cm) hatpin with clutch
- decorative beads
- one metal crimp bead
- small container of water
- Oriental or handmade paper
- Oriental fan shapelet or template of desired shape

- texture sheet
- gold Rub 'n Buff
- pasta machine
- acrylic roller
- craft knife
- tissue blade
- small piece of cardstock
- needle-nose pliers
- crimping pliers
- clay shaper tool

- superglue
- craft glue
- clear varnish
- pen
- scissors
- soft paintbrush
- paper towels

1. Moisten Clay
Condition 1 block of black clay and run it through the pasta machine on the #2 setting. Cut the sheet in half with a tissue blade and set half aside. Dip your fingers in water and moisten the prepared clay.

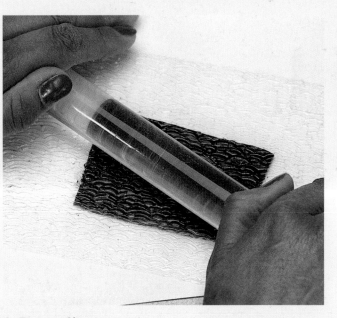

2. Texture Clay
Place a texture sheet or the material of your choice on the wet clay and roll back and forth firmly with an acrylic roller.

Tip

Water, like powder, works as a great release agent for clay.

3. Remove Clay
Carefully peel the clay from the texture sheet and blot off any excess water with a paper towel.

4. Cut Out Fan
Place the Oriental fan shapelet or the shape of your choice over the clay and cut it out with a craft knife. Bake for 20 minutes at 275° F (135° C). Allow to cool.

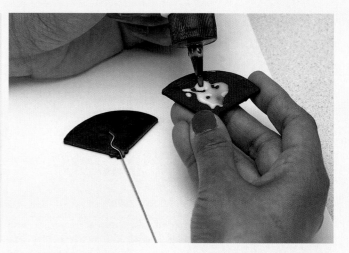

5. Repeat for Other Side
To make the other side of the pin, use the remaining untextured clay from step 1 to cut out another Oriental fan. Crimp, or zig-zag, ³⁄₄" (2cm) of the flattened end of the hatpin with needle-nose pliers and embed it into the raw clay.

6. Add Glue to Fan
Put a few drops of superglue on the crimped wire and the corners of the raw fan piece. Apply a thin coat of TLS on the back of the baked piece.

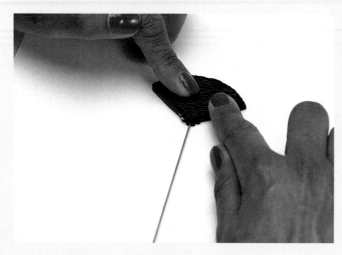

7. Adhere Baked and Raw Clay
Adhere the baked piece to the raw piece.

8. Smooth Edges
Smooth the outer edges of the fan with a clay shaper tool. Bake for 25 minutes at 275° F (135° C). Allow to cool.

9. Cut Out Paper Fan
Place the fan shapelet on Oriental or handmade decorative paper and trace the outline with a pen. Cut out the shape a tiny bit smaller than the outline.

10. Adhere Paper Fan
Apply a small amount of craft glue to the back of the paper and adhere it to the flat side of the baked fan.

11. Apply Metallic Finish
Squeeze a small dollop of gold Rub 'n Buff onto a piece of card-stock. Smear it with your finger to make a thin coating. Stroke your coated finger onto the textured side of the baked fan to highlight the raised areas. Allow to dry for 30 minutes.

12. Add Varnish and Beads
With a soft paintbrush, apply one coat of clear varnish over the metallic finish to seal it. Allow to dry. Slide decorative beads up the hatpin, supergluing each one in place. Finish with a metal crimping bead and flatten with crimping pliers to secure.

Mola Pendant

Watch these brilliant colors come to life as you carve away the top layer of black clay. Just imagine all the color combinations and patterns you can use to make this project a one-of-a-kind work of art!

MATERIALS

- ½ block each of red, orange, yellow, green and blue polymer clay or colors of your choice (Premo)
- 1 block of black polymer clay (Premo)
- liquid polymer clay (Translucent Liquid Sculpey [TLS])
- cane slices (optional)
- 2' (61cm) of rubber cord
- six O-rings
- 400- and 600-grit wet/dry sandpaper
- small container of water
- paper towels

- white colored pencil
- small piece of cardstock
- small piece of parchment paper
- superglue
- pasta machine
- acrylic roller
- tissue blade
- craft knife
- 2" (5cm) circular cutter
- V-gauge linoleum cutter (medium width) or carving tool
- stiff paintbrush

- soft cloth
- clay shaper tool
- needle tool
- small hand drill
- scissors
- bird pattern (page 122)

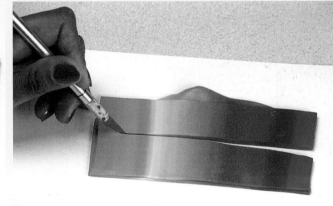

1. Prepare Clay
Make a rainbow blend from five assorted colors of clay (for instructions, see pages 18 - 19). Run the prepared rainbow sheet through the pasta machine on the #3 setting. Cut the sheet in half with a craft knife and stack one piece on top of the other with like colors touching.

2. Layer Clay
Repeat the cutting and stacking process to make four layers.

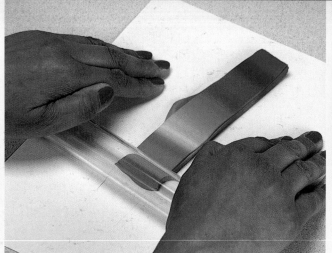

3. Taper End
Taper one of the narrow ends with an acrylic roller.

4. Roll Tapered End
Roll the tapered end, continuing until the entire strip is rolled. Smooth the seam with your finger.

5. Cut Slice of Clay
Cut a ¼" (6mm) slice from the roll with a tissue blade.

6. Flatten Slice
Gently flatten the slice with an acrylic roller and taper the outer edges with your fingers to make a dome shape.

7. Prepare and Add Black Clay

Condition 1 block of black clay and run it through the pasta machine on the #1 setting. Set ¾ of the clay aside for later use, and run the remaining clay through the pasta machine on the #7 setting. It will be paper-thin. Cover the rainbow dome with the thin black clay, pulling taut as you press.

8. Remove Air Bubbles

If you happen to get an air bubble, make a slit in the black clay with a craft knife and press out the air. Drag your finger over the slit to reseal.

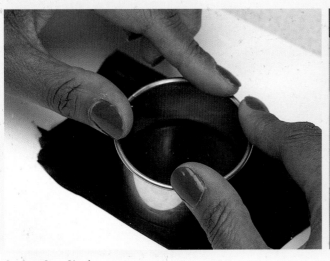

9. Cut Out Circle

Flatten the slice with an acrylic roller until it is about ⅛" (3mm) thick. Center a 2" (5cm) circular cutter over the piece and press down. Remove the excess clay. Bake for 30 minutes at 275° F (135° C). Allow to cool.

10. Sand Baked Clay

Presoak a sheet of 400-grit wet/dry sandpaper in water for a few minutes. Sand the baked piece with the sandpaper until smooth, dunking the piece into water occasionally as you sand.

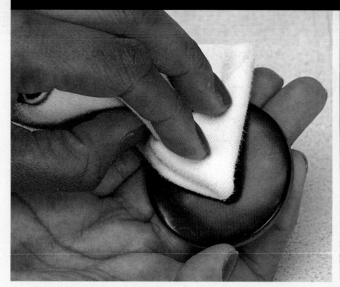

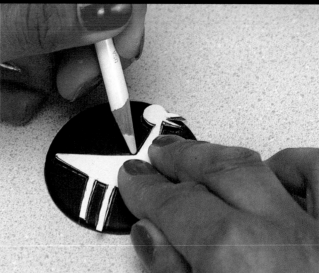

11. Dry and Buff Clay Piece
Blot the clay piece dry with a paper towel and buff to a satin finish with a soft cloth.

12. Trace Pattern
Cut out the bird pattern provided on page 122 or create your own and position it in the center of the baked clay piece. Trace the pattern with a white colored pencil.

13. Carve Along Lines
Skim a linoleum cutter or other carving tool along the white lines, rotating the piece as you go. Use cardstock or scrap paper as a turntable.

14. Continue Carving
Continue to carve as creatively as you like. The more you carve, the more color you will expose.

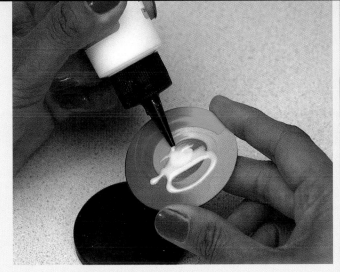

15. Adhere Raw Clay to Baked Clay

Run the remaining black clay from step 7 through the pasta machine on the #1 setting. Fold the clay to double the thickness. Cut out another circle with the 2" (5cm) circular cutter. Apply a thin coat of TLS and a few drops of superglue to the back of the baked clay piece and adhere it to the raw clay circle.

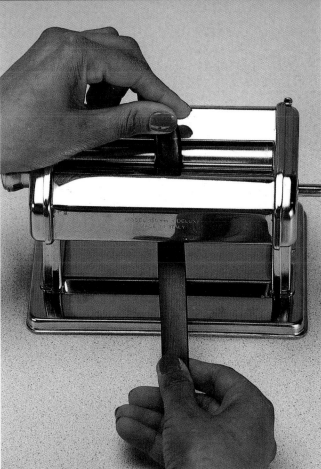

16. Make Strip for Border

To make a border for the pendant, begin by running the excess black clay from step 15 through the pasta machine on the #1 setting. The new strip should be long enough to wrap around the perimeter of the pendant.

17. Trim Border

Anchor the strip to your work surface and trim the width to approximately ³⁄₈" (1cm) or the width of your piece.

18. Wrap Strip Around Pendant
Starting at the bottom of the pendant, wrap the strip around the edge to form the border.

19. Trim Excess Clay
When you arrive at your starting point, trim the excess clay with a tissue blade. Seal the seam with your finger or a clay shaper tool.

20. Smooth Edges
Smooth the edges of the pendant by pressing down with a small piece of parchment paper. Texture the back of the piece or add cane slices as desired.

21. Sand Clay and Mark Holes
Use a needle tool to pierce holes in the top of the pendant, about 2" (5cm) apart and ½" (1cm) deep. Bake 30 minutes at 275° F (135° C). Allow to cool. Sand the top and sides of the pendant with 600-grit wet/dry sandpaper, dunking the piece into water occasionally as you did in step 10.

22. Drill Holes

With a small hand drill, drill a hole ½" (1cm) deep into both of the pierced holes in the pendant. The holes should be at least as wide as the rubber cord you will use to hang the pendant.

23. Prepare Cord

Measure the rubber cord to about 2' (60cm) long or the desired length and angle the ends with scissors. String three O-rings on each end.

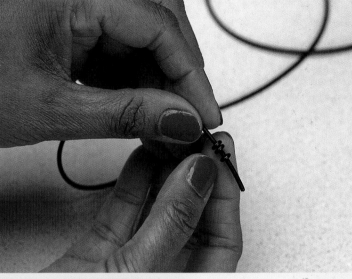

24. Add and Secure Cord

Apply a drop of superglue to each end of the cord and stick them into the holes. Hold them in place to dry for 20 seconds.

Mokume Gane Button

This beautiful Mokume Gane button project is great for using wooden Balinese stamps or deeply cut rubber stamps. Make an entire set, and update an old jacket or adorn a new one with your own custom-made creations. Challenge yourself to mix and match your own colors.

MATERIALS

- ½ block of taupe polymer clay; I mixed ⅜ block of ecru + ⅛ block of black (Premo)

- ½ block of light turquoise polymer clay; I mixed ⅜ block of turquoise + ⅛ block of ecru (Premo)

- ½ block of olive green polymer clay; I mixed ¼ block of black + ¼ block of gold (Premo)

- scraps of clay (equivalent to ½ block) in various colors

- liquid polymer clay (Translucent Liquid Sculpey [TLS])

- cane slices

- metal button shank

- mesh or lace

- button push mold

- pouncer (for instructions, see page 22)

- superglue

- 400- and 600-grit wet/dry sandpaper

- pasta machine

- tissue blade

- acrylic roller

- 2" (5cm) circular cutter

- craft knife

- stiff paintbrush

- needle tool

- soft cloth

1. Prepare Clay

Make a push mold in the desired shape of your buttons (for instructions, see page 22). Condition ½ block each of three contrasting colors of clay (I used taupe, light turquoise and olive green) and run through the pasta machine on the #3 setting. Trim each sheet to 3" x 4" (8cm x 10cm) with a tissue blade.

2. Taper and Layer Clay Sheets

Stack the sheets one on top of the other. Taper one end of the stack with an acrylic roller and run the sheet through the pasta machine on the #1 setting. Cut the sheet in half with a tissue blade and stack one half on top of the other, alternating colors, with cut edges together as shown. You now have six layers.

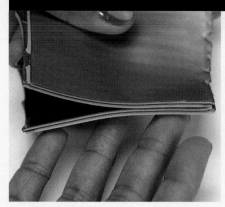

3. Continue Tapering and Layering

Taper the uncut edge and run the sheet through the pasta machine on the #1 setting again. Cut the sheet in half and stack again to form 12 layers. Taper the uncut end and run it through the pasta machine on the #2 setting. Cut in half and stack one final time. You now have 24 layers.

4. Impress Clay Into Mold

Trim the layered clay sheet to slightly larger than your prepared button mold. Set the excess clay aside for later use. Generously powder the clay with the pouncer (for pouncer instructions, see page 22). Powder your thumbs, too, so the clay won't stick to them. Press the clay piece against the mold firmly, making sure the clay spreads into each crevice.

5. Shape Button

Carefully peel the clay from the mold and trim around the edges with the circular cutter or craft knife to shape your button. Firmly press the outer edges of the button to anchor it to your work surface.

62

6. Reveal Underneath Layer

Use an extremely sharp tissue blade to skim the surface off the top of the button, revealing the layers underneath. Cut in a see-saw motion. Set the thin top layers aside for future jewelry projects.

7. Repeat Process

Repeat this process, bowing your blade to make sharp cuts, until the underneath layers are exposed in a decorative fashion. Be careful not to let them fall back down into the crevices. Re-trim the edges of the button if necessary. For a satin finish, sand the top and sides of the button with 400- and 600-grit wet/dry sandpaper, then buff with a soft cloth. Bake for 20 minutes at 275° F (135° C).

Tip

Use the thin layers you cut off the button to decorate a sheet of clay in a contrasting color.

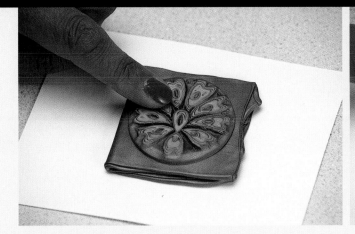

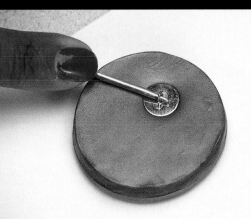

8. Prepare Back of Button

To make the back of the button, run a scrap of clay in a coordinating color through the pasta machine on the #1 setting. Fold the sheet in half, making sure it is at least as wide as your button. Apply a thin coat of TLS to the back of the baked piece, then add a few drops of superglue. Adhere to the raw piece and press down firmly for 20 seconds.

9. Adhere Button Shank

Trim the excess clay from around the button with a craft knife. Add a drop of superglue to a metal button shank and adhere it to the upper third of the button back. Press firmly with a needle tool for 20 seconds to allow the glue to dry.

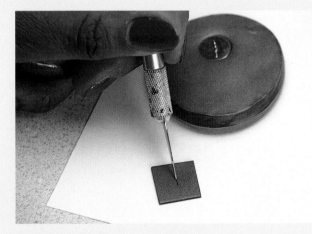

10. Conceal Shank

Use a cane slice or cut a small shape out of scrap clay to conceal the shank. Use a craft knife to cut a slit in the clay long enough to fit over the shank.

11. Adhere Clay to Shank

Add a few drops of superglue to the front of the shank and slip the clay shape into place. Use mesh or lace to texture the backing. Bake 45 minutes at 275° F (135° C). Allow to cool.

Tip

Wouldn't it be nice to have a brooch to match your buttons? Follow the steps for making a button, but attach a pin back instead of a button shank. For instructions on how to attach a pin back, see steps 16 and 17 on page 31.

Textures Gallery

Feathered Hatpins

I designed this pair of hatpins with alternating combinations of black and white clay. Once baked, the pieces were carved to reveal the underlying layer. I made an opening at the top of each piece so the feathers could be inserted and glued. The glass beads complete the composition.

Hinged Pendant

I love how the many textures in this pendant complement each other. The carved olive green and simulated turquoise pieces were mounted onto a coral base textured with a wire mesh screen. This component was attached to a carved, hinged section. African brass beads and mizuhiki cord embellish this pendant.

Cowrie Shell Brooch

I USED A SNAKESKIN RUBBER STAMP TO TEXTURE THE NEUTRAL COLORS OF CLAY IN THIS BROOCH. THE LARGE COWRIE SHELL WAS EMBEDDED INTO THE BASE, THEN SURROUNDED WITH FOLDED SHEETS OF CLAY. THE APPLICATION OF METALLIC POWDERS GIVES THIS BROOCH AN ELEGANT APPEARANCE.

Carved Hatpin

FOR THIS PIECE, I COVERED A THICK CANE SLICE WITH A THIN SHEET OF BLACK CLAY AND BAKED IT. THE TECHNIQUE OF SCRATCHING THROUGH ONE COLOR TO GET TO ANOTHER, KNOWN IN THE POTTERY WORLD AS "SGRAFFITO," REVEALS THE MULTIPLE COLORS UNDERNEATH. I ADDED MATCHING GLASS BEADS TO ACCENT THE PIECE.

African Mask Pendant

TO MAKE THIS PENDANT, I MADE A MOLD FROM AN AFRICAN BRASS MASK EMBELLISHMENT, THEN COATED IT WITH METALLIC POWDER. ONCE BAKED, I MOUNTED THE PIECE ONTO A SHEET OF CLAY TEXTURED WITH THICK WIRE MESH SCREEN AND COATED WITH BLUE METALLIC POWDER. BRASS AND GLASS BEADS DANGLE FROM THE PENDANT TO ADD MOVEMENT.

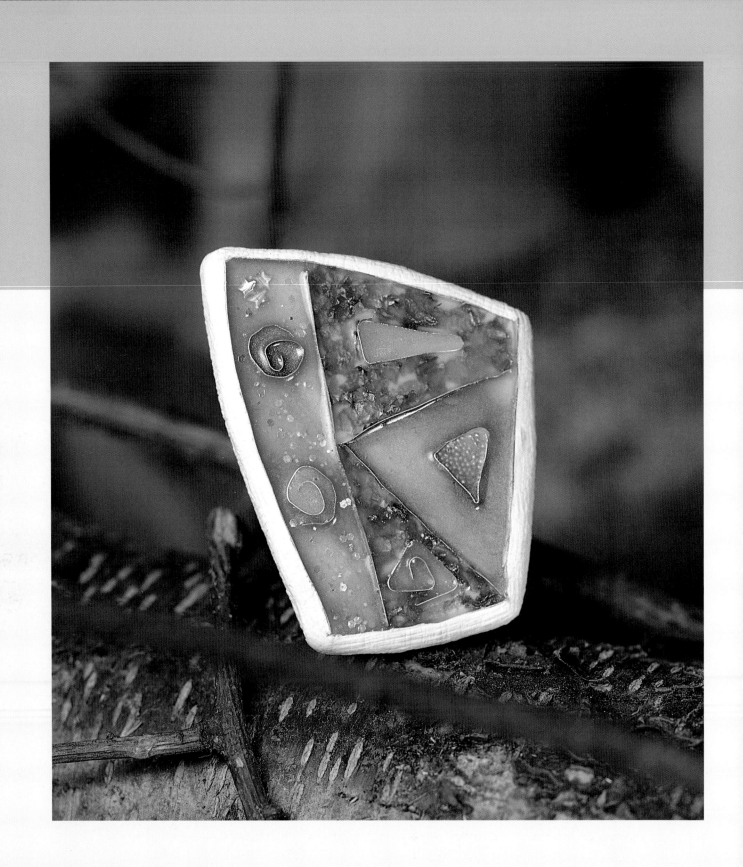

Liquid Polymer Clay

Liquid polymer clay is a fabulous product. I use it to make photo transfers, fill in gaps, strengthen thin areas, seal gold leaf or painted surfaces, laminate decorative materials, attach baked clay to raw clay—I could go on and on!

Liquid polymer clay is not glue (as often thought), so it won't adhere two pieces of clay together and set when dry. Since it is clay, it must still be baked to ensure that the pieces stick to each other. There are two brands I keep on hand and have used for the projects in this book. They are Translucent Liquid Sculpey (TLS) and Kato Liquid Polyclay clear medium. I have found that TLS has a semitransparent appearance at times, while Kato Liquid Polyclay has a clear, glasslike appearance when baked. In this section, you'll learn how to use this versatile medium in some creative ways.

When it comes to seed beads, I have found an easier way of working with them right off the hank! The Embedded Bead Earrings were quick and simple to make, as you'll find on page 68. I used TLS as grout to pull the whole composition together.

The Eggshell Mosaic Brooch (page 72), a mosaic project, is so much fun! I really enjoyed experimenting with different dyes, and I discovered that food coloring, inks and fabric dyes work well. The contrasting grout, made with colored TLS, helps to define the patterns.

The Laminated Collage Pendant (page 74) comes from my love of making collages. The art of "cutting and pasting" is relaxing because there are almost no rules. The only rule I can think of is that you must know when it is time to stop. Otherwise, you might get carried away with this project.

The cloisonné technique is one in which silver or gold wire is bent to form designs. Enamel is then laid into the resulting chambers, or "cloisons." For the Faux Cloisonné Enamel Brooch (page 78), you'll learn how to apply one thin coat of liquid polymer clay at a time with multiple bakings to create a glassy look of enamel.

Embedded Bead Earrings

These simple, yet tasteful, pearl and glass beaded earrings have a luminescent radiance. You can even try experimenting with other patterns and bead combinations with this technique. This is also a great way to use small, loose beads.

The steps in this project will complete one earring. It is quicker to make the pair simultaneously so that by the end of the last step, both will be completed.

MATERIALS

- 1/2 block of aqua clay; I mixed 1/4 block of sea green + 1/4 block of white (Premo)
- liquid polymer clay (Translucent Liquid Sculpey [TLS])
- two freshwater pearls
- hank of glass beads (I cut off two strands)
- metallic powder
- earring posts
- lace or texture material
- superglue
- small piece of paper
- pasta machine
- 1" x 3/4" (3cm x 1.9cm) oval cutter
- scissors
- needle tool
- plastic container
- stirring stick
- soft cloth
- stiff paintbrush
- clay shaper tool

1. Adhere Pearl to Oval
Condition 1/2 block of aqua clay and run it through the pasta machine on the #3 setting. Cut out a circle with a 1" x 3/4" (3cm x 1.9cm) oval cutter. Place a drop of superglue on a freshwater pearl and place it in the center of the oval. Press for 20 seconds.

2. Anchor Pearl Strand
Cut off an 18" (46cm) strand of glass beads and superglue each end to secure the beads on the string. Put a drop of superglue on the base of the pearl and anchor the end of the strand to the pearl with a needle tool.

3. Wrap Strand Around Pearl

Circle the pearl with the strand of beads, pushing down with a needle tool or lacing tool as you go. Wrap until the entire surface is covered, including the edges, using a small piece of paper as a turntable.

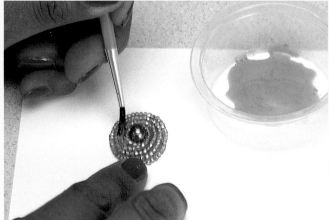

4. Finish Outline and Trim Strand

Superglue the last bead to the clay and allow it to dry before trimming the strand. It is not necessary to glue the entire strand since the clay is raw, but glue in spots if necessary.

5. Color Liquid Polymer Clay

Squeeze about one teaspoon of TLS into a container and stir in a pinch of metallic powder until the desired color is achieved.

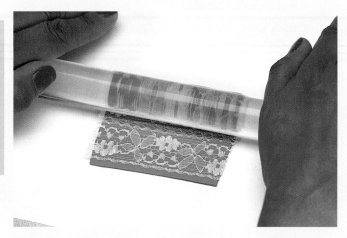

6. Paint Liquid Polymer Clay Over Beads

Using a stiff paintbrush, paint the metallic TLS mixture between the rows of beads to fill the crevices. Wipe away excess with a soft cloth. Bake for 20 minutes at 275° F (135° C). Allow to cool.

Tip

When coloring liquid polymer clay, it takes only a small amount of metallic powder to achieve the desired effect.

7. Texture Clay

Texture the remaining clay from step 1 with lace or the material of your choice.

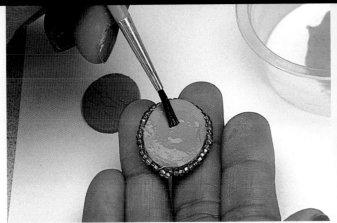

8. Add Earring Back

To make the earring back, cut out another oval from the textured clay. Paint a light coat of the remaining metallic mixture onto the back of the baked piece. This will cause it to adhere after baking. Press gently and smooth the edges with your finger or a clay shaper tool.

9. Adhere Post

Superglue an earring post to the upper half of the raw clay. Press for 20 seconds.

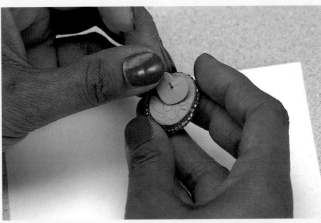

10. Prepare Scrap Clay

Run a small piece of scrap clay through the pasta machine on the #5 setting. Cut out a small circle or any shape large enough to conceal the earring base.

11. Conceal Base

Pierce a hole in the center of the raw clay shape. Add a drop of superglue the top of the metal earring base and slide the clay shape down the post. Smooth the edges.

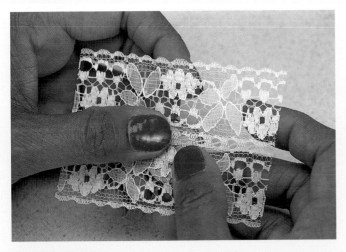

12. Texture Base

Compress the raw clay over the base with lace to add texture and secure the clay. Place earrings bead-side down on polyester batting on a baking sheet. Bake for 25 minutes at 275° F (135° C).

Eggshell Mosaic Brooch

Artistic mosaics can be made with just about any material — even eggshells! To dye the shells with food coloring, mix 3 tablespoons of hot water, 1 teaspoon of food coloring and ½ teaspoon of vinegar. To dye the shells with fabric dye, mix 1 teaspoon of powder or liquid dye with 3 tablespoons of cold water. Peel and rinse the shells from several hard-boiled eggs, and soak them in the desired dye until your color is achieved. Strain the dye from the eggshells and rinse thoroughly with cold water. Place the eggshells on a paper towel to dry.

MATERIALS

- 1 block of light-colored polymer clay (Premo)
- translucent liquid polymer clay (Translucent Liquid Sculpey [TLS])
- cane slices
- prepared eggshell pieces in various colors
- metallic powder, any color
- pin back
- black colored pencil
- superglue
- pasta machine
- scissors
- paintbrush
- small plastic container
- tissue blade
- stirring stick
- soft cloth
- pattern (page 122)

1. Transfer Pattern (Top Left)

Condition 1 block of light-colored clay and run it through the pasta machine on the #3 setting. Cut out the pattern from page 122 and draw a design inside the pattern. Trace the pattern and design with a black colored pencil and press it facedown on the clay to transfer the image. Burnish with your fingers. Remove the pattern and cut the shape out of the clay with a tissue blade.

2. Add Eggshells (Top Right)

Spread a thin coat of TLS onto the clay with a paintbrush. Dip the paintbrush into the TLS and pick up the eggshells with the wet brush. Apply the shells to the raw clay, using the design as your guide. Leave hairline spaces between the shells. Bake 20 minutes at 275° F (135° C). Allow to cool.

3. Add Grout and Finish Piece

In a small container, mix 1 teaspoon of TLS with the metallic powder of your choice. Paint "grout" over the mosaic, making sure the mixture goes in between the shells. Blot the excess grout with a soft cloth. Bake for 10 minutes at 275° F (135° C). Allow to cool. To make the back, run ½ block of leftover clay through the pasta machine on the #2 setting. Cut out a shape slightly larger than the baked piece. Spread TLS on the back of the baked piece and mount it to the raw piece. Superglue a pin back to the upper third of the back and cover with cane slices to conceal. Bake mosaic-side down for 25 minutes at 275° F (135° C). Allow to cool.

Tip

Mimic the pattern of your eggshell mosaic brooch to make matching earrings. For instructions on how to embed French hook ear wires, see pages 94-95, steps 18-22.

Laminated Collage Pendant

Are you tired of chasing gold leaf that flies away? Well, chase no more! You can strengthen leaf and a variety of other materials with liquid polymer clay. This enables you to cut it with scissors and have full control of your shapes. This project invites you to compose an abstract or realistic free-form collage.

To prepare for this project, laminate metallic leaf, fabric and assorted papers as described on pages 20-21.

MATERIALS

- ¹/₂ block of gold polymer clay (Premo)

- 1 block of turquoise polymer clay (Premo)

- liquid polymer clay (Translucent Liquid Sculpey [TLS])

- gold leaf flakes

- various laminated materials

- 2mm black imitation leather cord, 26" (66cm) long

- necklace clasp

- wire mesh screen

- pouncer (for instructions, see page 22)

- superglue

- pasta machine

- paintbrush

- acrylic roller

- scissors

- tissue blade

- pattern (page 123)

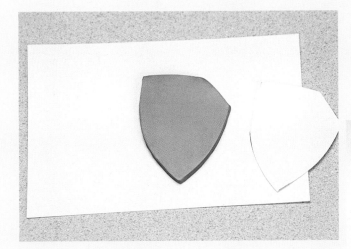

1. Cut Out Clay Piece
Condition 1 block of gold clay and run it through the pasta machine on the #1 setting. Cut out the pattern on page 123 and place it on the clay piece. Use a tissue blade to cut out the shape. Set the excess clay aside for later use.

2. Apply Gold Leaf
Apply small flakes of gold leaf randomly onto the raw clay, pressing gently as you go.

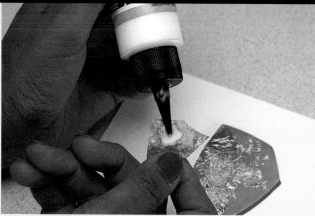

3. Cut Out Laminated Shapes
Select a piece of laminated metallic leaf and cut out random shapes with craft scissors as desired.

4. Apply Liquid Polymer Clay
Apply a thin coat of TLS to the backs of the laminated shapes and spread evenly with a paintbrush.

5. Impress Into Clay
Press with your fingers to adhere the shapes randomly to the raw clay piece.

6. Continue Adding Laminated Shapes
Continue this process using laminated sheets of various materials. Bake your finished piece for 20 minutes at 275° F (135° C). Allow to cool.

7. Make Frame and Backing
To make the frame and backing, condition 1 block of turquoise clay and run it through the pasta machine on #1 setting. Lightly powder both sides of the clay and wipe away any excess. Add texture by "sandwiching" the clay between wire mesh or the material of your choice. Roll with an acrylic roller to impress.

8. Adhere Raw Clay to Baked Clay

Trim around the edges of the raw clay, leaving a border that is larger than the baked piece. Apply TLS to the back of the baked piece and place it in the center of the raw clay.

9. Make Curved Cuts

Make curved cuts by bowing the tissue blade and pressing straight down on both ends. Be sure to leave a 1" (3cm) extension at the top for the "bail," or the hoop-like support on a pendant through which the cord is threaded.

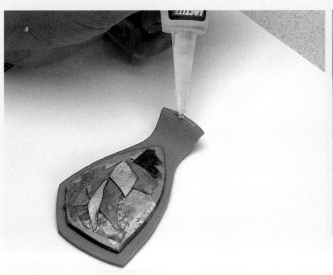

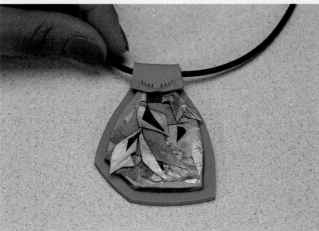

10. Bend Down Extension

Superglue a thin line across the top edge of the extension and bend it down, leaving an opening for the cord. This forms the bail. Texture the portion of the bail that meets the pendant with a leather stamping tool or texturing tool of your choice. Bake for 30 minutes at 275° F (135° C). Allow to cool.

11. Thread the Cord

Thread the cord through the hole of the bail and add a few drops of superglue inside the bail to keep the cord in place. Finish the necklace with a clasp or tie as desired.

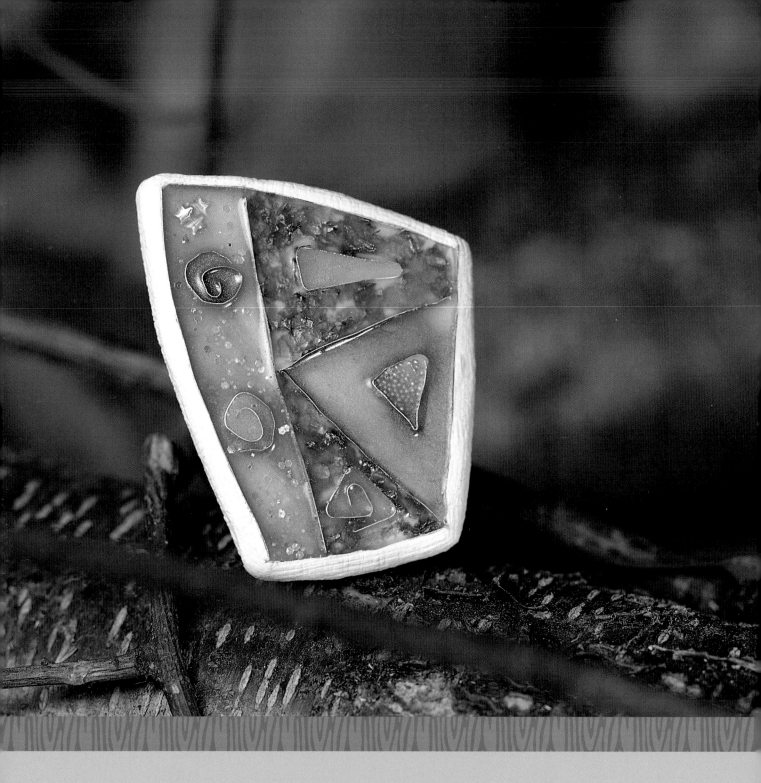

Faux Cloisonné Enamel Brooch

Upgrade your work by using fine silver wire. This elegant piece comes remarkably close to the real thing! I used Kato Liquid Polyclay clear medium for this project, which gives the brooch a glasslike appearance.

MATERIALS

- 1 block of white polymer clay (Premo)
- Kato Liquid Polyclay clear medium
- cane slices
- 16" (40.6cm) of fine silver cloisonné wire, 1.50mm x 0.13mm
- metallic leaf flakes
- tiny glass balls without holes
- 1¼" (0.6cm) pin back

- stardust glitter
- lace or texture material
- black colored pencil
- superglue
- craft glue
- pasta machine
- small piece of paper
- scissors
- craft knife
- needle tool
- soft paintbrush

- plastic containers
- stirring sticks
- clay shaper tool
- flat acrylic sheet
- pattern (page 123)
- wire cutters
- needle-nose pliers

1. Cut out Clay Shape with Pattern

Condition 1 block of white clay and run it through the pasta machine on the #1 setting. Cut out the pattern provided on page 123 and trace the design with a black colored pencil. Place the pattern design-side down on the clay and rub it with your fingers to transfer the image onto the clay. Trace around the template with your craft knife and set the excess clay aside for later use.

2. Reveal Pattern

Lift off the pattern to reveal the transferred image.

3. Score Channels Into Clay
Score the pattern with a needle tool to make shallow channels to embed the cloisonné wire. Continue to score the outside circumference of the brooch within $1/16"$ (2mm) from the edge.

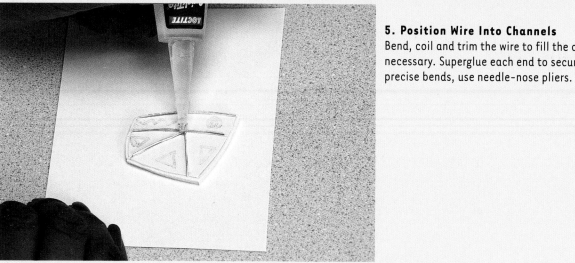

4. Embed Wire
Hold the cloisonné wire up to the channels to approximate the appropriate length you will need. Cut the wire to the desired length with wire cutters. Embed the cloisonné wire into the channels with your fingers or a needle tool.

Tip

For a firmer wire, try using silver or gold-filled bezel wire instead of cloisonné wire.

5. Position Wire Into Channels
Bend, coil and trim the wire to fill the channels as necessary. Superglue each end to secure. For more precise bends, use needle-nose pliers.

6. Apply Metallic Leaf

Apply flakes of metallic leaf in the chambers between the wire. Pat down with a paintbrush. The metallic leaf will stick to the raw clay.

7. Add Tiny Glass Balls

Add Kato Liquid Polyclay clear medium to one of the remaining chambers, filling it half-way. Pour a scoop of tiny glass balls into the chamber and use a needle tool to arrange them if necessary.

8. Fill Remaining Chambers

Mix ½ teaspoon of Kato medium and a pinch of metallic powder in a small container. Make several of these mixtures in various colors. Apply medium-thick coats of the tinted Kato medium into the remaining chambers. Bake for 15 minutes at 275º F (135º C). Allow to cool.

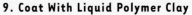

9. Coat With Liquid Polymer Clay

Squeeze more Kato medium over the metallic leaf and beads to coat. Fill to the edge of the wire and spread with a paintbrush. Apply a generous second coat of tinted Kato medium to the chambers. Add glitter and other additives as desired. Fill until the liquid is level with the wire. Bake for 20 minutes at 275° F (135° C). Allow to cool.

10. Make Frame

To frame the piece, run the remaining clay from step 1 through the pasta machine on the #3 setting. Texture the clay with lace or the material of your choice. Place the clay textured-side down and brush the back of the baked piece with clear Kato medium. Place the baked piece in the middle of the raw clay and press firmly to adhere.

11. Trim Around Edges

Use a craft knife to trim 1/4" (6mm) wider than the actual piece. Set the excess clay aside.

12. Adhere Frame to Baked Piece

Outline the edges of the baked piece with craft glue. Bend the raw clay edges up and around the sides of the baked piece. Smooth the seam with your finger or a clay shaper tool.

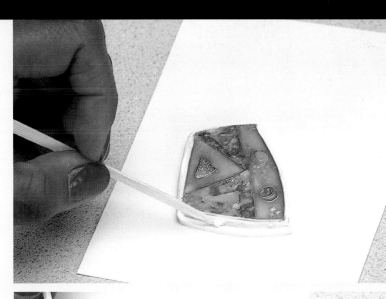

13. Wrap Snake Around Piece

Use the excess clay from step 11 to roll out a snake long enough to wrap around the entire baked piece. Anchor the edge of the snake with a drop of superglue, and trace around the piece to create a border. Press firmly with your fingers and trim off any excess.

14. Flatten Edges

Flatten the outer edge to the same height as the wire by pressing down with a flat acrylic sheet. Add texture with lace or the material of your choice. To finish, superglue a pin back to the upper third of the brooch and cover the bar with cane slices or a thin sheet of clay. Place the brooch on a baking sheet, enamel-side down. Bake for 25 minutes at 275° F (135° C). Allow to cool.

Eggshell Mosaic Brooches

THE EGGSHELLS I USED TO MAKE THIS TRIO OF BROOCHES WERE COLORED WITH INKS, FOOD COLORING AND FABRIC DYES. I ARRANGED THE FRAGMENTS INTO MOSAIC PATTERNS ON CLAY COATED WITH TLS. METALLIC-TINTED TLS MAKES UP THE GROUT. THE DIMENSIONAL BROOCH ON THE LEFT HAS LEAF CANES AND CLAY EXTRUSIONS CUT AND BUNDLED FOR THE CENTER OF THE FLOWER. METALLIC GLASS BEADS WERE USED IN THE BROOCH ON THE RIGHT TO SEPARATE THE MOSAIC SEGMENTS.

84

Laminated Brooch

I MADE THIS BROOCH WITH MULTIPLE LAYERS OF FABRIC LAMINATED WITH TLS AND MOUNTED ON A TEXTURED BASE WITH CRACKED SILVER LEAF. I THEN STRUNG MIZUHIKI CORD THROUGH BAKED POLYMER DISCS FOR ADDED DETAIL.

Beaded Brooch

FRESHWATER PEARLS, BUGLE BEADS, A WIRE COIL AND STRUNG GLASS BEADS MAKE UP THIS BEADED "COLLAGE" BROOCH. THE BEADS WERE EMBEDDED INTO A MIXTURE OF GOLD AND BLACK PREMO AND GROUTED WITH TLS TINTED WITH AN ANTIQUE GOLD METALLIC POWDER.

Faux Cloisonné Enamel Brooch

Here, I filled fine silver bezel wire cells with layers of Kato Liquid Polyclay clear medium tinted with metallic powder. The mixture is applied over silver leaf and red paper. I used black and silver gel pens to draw patterns between the layers. I love how they appear to float on the surface.

Faux Cloisonné Enamel Pendant

For this piece, I baked Kato Liquid Polyclay clear medium into the fine silver bezel wire cells filled with copper leaf, black polymer clay pieces, glass balls and 24-karat gold leaf flakes. The Buna cord with O-rings adds an additional point of interest.

Pair of Faux Cloisonné Enamel Brooches

For the brooch on the left, fine silver bezel wire was embedded into the clay. I applied lightly tinted Kato Liquid Polyclay clear medium and layered it with fine copper mesh screen, copper leaf and 24-karat gold leaf flakes.

I made the brooch on the right by embedding fine silver cloisonné wire into the clay, then baking the piece. The "cloisons," or cells, were filled with metallic powders, gold leaf and tiny glass balls, then covered with Kato Liquid Polyclay clear medium.

Canes

A cane is made from two or more colors of clay attached together in ways that create a continual pattern when sliced throughout. You can make a simple checkerboard, spiral, striped or bull's-eye cane from a log, snake or sheet. One of the first things that attracted me to polymer clay was seeing these colorful, intricate, repeated patterns on beads and other items. The fascination aroused my curiosity, so I began to explore this interesting medium by making my own canes.

While I'm not a master cane-maker, I have begun to look at everyday patterns in a new light. I challenge myself to mimic textile motifs, animal prints, nature forms and architectural designs in my canes. The projects in this section include some of these creations.

When it comes to leaf shapes, the ginkgo leaf is my favorite. It is one of the few leaves that is shaped like a fan. Although the ginkgo leaf is usually a solid color, I invented a cane with a slight color gradation to give it more depth for the Ginkgo Leaf Earrings (page 88).

Taking pride in my culture, I have been collecting African textiles for years. I love the richness of color in Kente cloth and indigo, and the earth tones and textures of Kuba cloth and mudcloth. After carefully studying the patterns in these textiles, I challenged myself to create canes of each. I'm happy to share one with you in the Mudcloth Pendant project (page 102).

I have had great fun teaching classes on how to make animal print canes. Each week, we studied a different animal pattern and constructed a cane to be used in jewelry-making or home decorating projects. Here I've included three wonderful animal print cane projects for you to try: the Snakeskin Bangle (page 96), the Bengal Tiger Brooch (page 110) and the Sea Turtle Pendant (page 116).

I hope you will enjoy making the canes in this chapter. The many color combinations and project possibilities will keep you going for days!

Ginkgo Leaf Earrings

These earrings have a delicate appearance, but they are strong and lightweight to wear. You can even experiment with other color combinations for various effects.

Note that the steps in this project will complete one earring. It is quicker to make the pair simultaneously, so both will be completed by the end of the last step.

MATERIALS

- ½ block of light green polymer clay; I mixed ³/8 block of champagne + ⅛ block of leaf green (Fimo Classic)

- ½ block of medium green polymer clay; I mixed ³/8 block of leaf green + ⅛ block of champagne (Fimo Classic)

- ¼ block of dark green polymer clay; I mixed ¼ block of leaf green + a tiny bit of black (Fimo Classic)

- two 1" (3cm) eye pins

- two French hook ear wires

- pasta machine

- acrylic roller

- tissue blade

- needle tool

- wire cutters

- needle-nose pliers

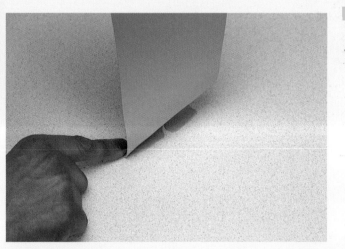

1. Prepare Clay
Make a Skinner blend with ½ block of light green clay and ½ block of medium green clay (for instructions, see pages 16–17). Place the lightest edge of the blended clay sheet in the pasta machine and run it through on the #3 setting. Continue to run the sheet through on the #4, #5 and #6 settings, starting with the lightest end. This will make it a long, thin strip.

2. Begin Accordion Fold
Anchor the lightest end of the strip to your work surface and hold up the dark end. Accordion-fold the strip, using your finger to press down each crease. The base of the accordion fold should measure approximately ½" (1cm).

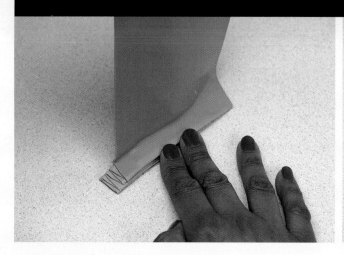

3. Finish Accordion Fold
Fold the entire strip of clay in this manner.

4. Reveal Cane
When completely folded, the strip will look like a pleated bar. This is now called a "cane."

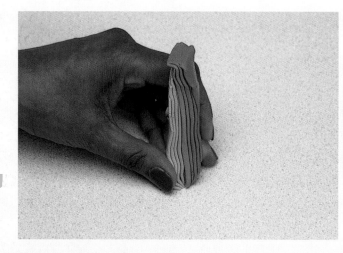

5. Form a Rectangle
Press in the ends of the cane firmly to form a rectangular bar. Square up the elongated edges of the cane with an acrylic roller.

6. Prepare Cane Wrap
Run ¼ block of dark green clay through the pasta machine on the #7 setting. Trim off any ragged edges with a tissue blade. Position the accordion cane on the edge of the flattened sheet.

Tip

When you need a very thin sheet of clay such as a #6 or #7, it is best to gradually work your way down to it. Start with a #1 setting, move to #3, #5, then #6 or #7. These steps prevent the clay from becoming distorted too quickly.

7. Wrap Around Cane

Roll the dark green sheet around the cane until the entire cane is wrapped. Trim off the excess clay from the sheet and set it aside for later use.

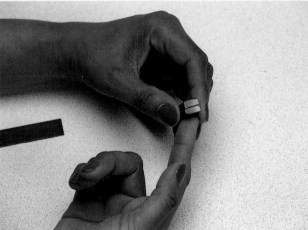

8. Compress Cane

Place the cane on its side with both the light and medium colors against your work surface as shown. Compress the cane with an acrylic roller until both ends are rectangular.

9. Reduce Cane

Pull, stretch and roll the clay, flattening as you go, maintaining the rectangular shape, to reduce the cane to 16" (41cm). Reducing the cane refers to reducing the design by stretching and compressing the cane.

10. Cut and Stack Cane

Trim 1" (3cm) from each end with a tissue blade. Cut the cane in half and stack one half on top of the other. The light colors on the inside of the cane should be facing the same direction.

Tip

If you ever reduce your cane too far, simply push the ends back toward each other.

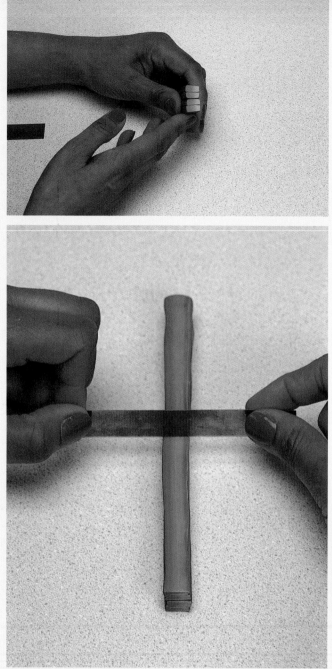

11. Cut, Stack and Reduce Cane
Cut the cane in half and stack it again to make four layers. Reduce the cane to 10" (25cm) as described in step 9. Flatten the cane as you go.

12. Repeat Cutting, Stacking and Reducing
Cut the flattened cane in half with a tissue blade and stack again. You will now have eight layers, which form the "veins" of the leaf cane.

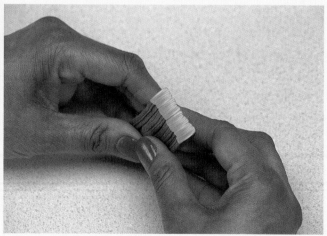

13. Repeat Process Again
Reduce the cane to 12" (30cm), cut it in half and stack it. Repeat cutting and stacking once more to reveal 32 blended segments, separated by veins.

14. Pinch Cane Into Wedge
Place the cane dark-side down on your work surface. Pinch it into a triangular wedge.

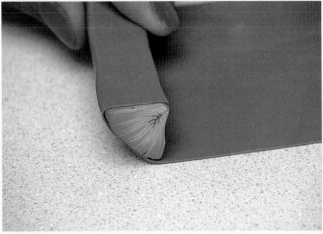

15. Wrap Wedge
Using the excess dark green clay from step 7, wrap the sheet once around the triangular wedge and trim off the remainder.

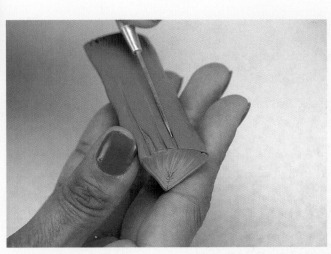

16. Create Crevices
Drag a needle tool across the top of the wedge to form crevices.

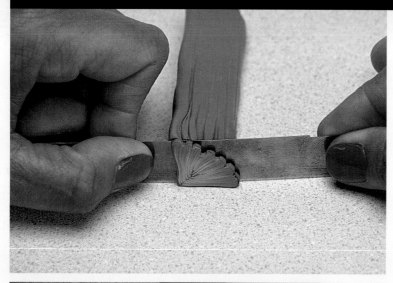

17. Cut Slices
Cut two $1/16$" (2mm) slices from the ginkgo leaf wedge with a tissue blade.

18. Prepare Eye Pin
Trim the eye pin to $1/2$" (1cm) with wire cutters if necessary. Grip the top of the eye pin tightly with your fingers. Place the straight end in the tips of your needle-nose pliers and zigzag the wire to crimp it. This will help to secure the eye pin in the clay.

19. Position Eye Pin
Position the eye pin in the center of the raw clay slice and press it into place with a needle tool.

20. Conceal Eye Pin

Place the remaining leaf slice on top of the eye pin to conceal it and seal the edges with your finger. Bake for 30 minutes at 275° F (135° C). Allow to cool.

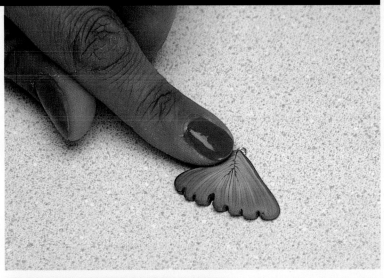

21. Open French Loop

Slightly open the loop of the French hook ear wire sideways with needle-nose pliers.

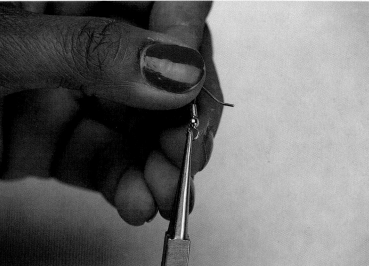

22. Attach Earring

Attach the earring and pinch the wire shut with pliers.

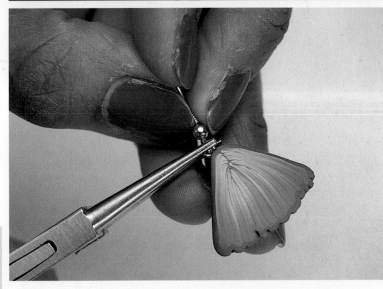

Tip

Apply slices from your ginkgo leaf cane onto a textured piece of scrap clay to make a beautiful matching brooch. Add a pin back as shown on page 31, steps 16-17, and bake as directed.

Snakeskin Bangle

A demonstration at my polymer clay guild got me thinking about snakeskin, so I bought some heavy mesh screen and started to experiment. Although I am not into snakes, I have found that their colors and patterns are beautiful. Translucent clay and metallic leaf add another dimension to this multilayered cane, and fluorescent clays make the colors pop. This bangle has hidden elastic so you can slip it on and off with ease. Make one or several to wear as a set.

MATERIALS

- 1 block of translucent polymer clay (Premo)

- $5/8$ block of translucent sea green polymer clay; I mixed $1/2$ block of sea green + $1/8$ block of translucent (Premo)

- $5/8$ block of translucent copper polymer clay; I mixed $1/2$ block of copper + $1/8$ block of translucent (Premo)

- $5/8$ block of olive green polymer clay; I mixed $1/4$ block of black + $1/4$ block of gold + $1/8$ block of translucent (Premo)

- $5/8$ block of chartreuse green polymer clay; I mixed $1/4$ block of zinc yellow + $1/8$ block of fluorescent yellow + $1/8$ block of sea green + $1/8$ block translucent (Premo)

- gold leaf

- 2mm round elastic

- wire mesh gutter screen

- 400- and 600-grit wet/dry sandpaper

- superglue

- pasta machine

- craft knife

- tissue blade

- acrylic roller

- wax paper

- needle tool

- double-pointed knitting needle

- 10" (25.4cm) bamboo skewer

- ruler

- clay shaper tool

- buffing wheel or soft cloth

- round glass jar or can

1. Prepare Clay Sheets

Condition 1 block of translucent clay and run it through the pasta machine on the #5 setting. Next, run each of the mixed colors listed above through on the #3 setting. Trim the prepared sheets to $2^{1}/2$" x 3" (6cm x 8cm) with a tissue blade.

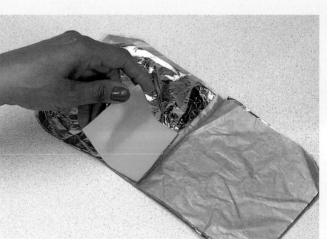

2. Apply Gold Leaf

Place each colored clay sheet on top of a piece of gold leaf. Trim off the excess with a craft knife. Flip the sheets over so the gold leaf is on top.

Tip

When working with gold leaf, it's wise to leave it in the package for better control. Remember to always place your clay on the leaf, not the leaf on your clay.

3. Stack Clay Sheets

Cut the prepared sheet of translucent clay into four rectangles measuring 2½" x 3" (6cm x 8cm) each. Place each translucent sheet on top of the four gold leaf sheets. Stack the sheets on top of each other with the translucent clay facing up.

4. Reduce and Layer Stack

Reduce the stack to 6" x 2½" (15cm x 6cm) by pulling, stretching and rolling with an acrylic roller. Cut the stack in half with the tissue blade and place one half on top of the other with cut edges touching.

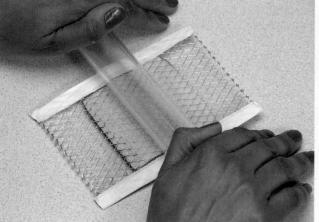

5. Texture Stack

Lightly powder the top of the clay and impress wire mesh (I used Gutter Guard, available at your local hardware store) or the material of your choice into the stack with an acrylic roller. Carefully remove the wire mesh and set it aside.

6. Shave Off Top

Bow your sharpest, most flexible tissue blade and trim off long, paper-thin slices in a seesaw motion. Flip the slices over onto a sheet of wax paper to reveal the pattern. Continue slicing, adding more texture with the screen as necessary.

Tip

It is not necessary to slice the entire stack. Slice only the amount you may need for each project and save the rest for another piece.

7. Make Clay Ball

Combine some of the excess clay from the colored sheets in step 1 (the equivalent of $1/2$ block) and roll it into a ball. Pierce a hole all the way through the ball with a needle tool.

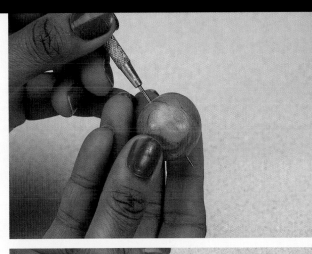

8. Roll Ball Into Snake

Insert a double-pointed knitting needle into the hole. Form a long tube, or snake, around the needle by rolling and stretching the clay, using even pressure with both hands.

9. Trim Snake to Desired Length

Determine the size of your bracelet by wrapping a string or strip of paper around your wrist and adding 1" (3cm). Transfer the snake to a bamboo skewer and roll to the desired length. Use a ruler for precise measurement. Trim off the edges with a tissue blade.

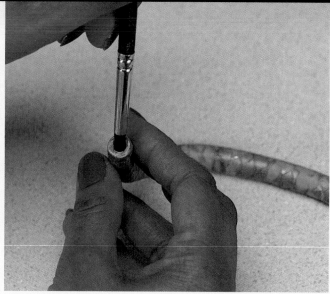

10. Apply Thin Slices

Select thin slices from step 6 and gently apply them to the snake in random patterns. Overlap and leave open spaces as desired, covering the circumference of the snake. Roll the snake to smooth the outer surface, trimming the ends if necessary.

11. Widen Holes

Slide the snake off the bamboo skewer and widen the holes on each end with a clay shaper tool.

12. Shape Snake Into Oval

Attach the ends of the snake to each other and seal the seam gently with your finger. Shape the snake into an oval bracelet, making sure the seam is at the widest point. Bake for 30 minutes at 275° F (135° C). Allow to cool.

13. Sand and Buff Bracelet

Sand the bracelet with 400- and 600-grit sandpaper and buff with a buffing tool or a soft cloth. Place the bracelet back in the oven for 5 minutes to make it warm and flexible.

14. Cut Bracelet in Half

While the bracelet is still warm and flexible, use a tissue blade to cut it in half lengthwise. Use a craft knife to enlarge one of the holes.

15. Add Elastic

Cut a piece of elastic to measure about 4" (10cm) longer than the bracelet. Thread the elastic through both halves and tie the ends together in a secure double knot. Reopen the bracelet and place a few drops of superglue on the knot. Allow to dry.

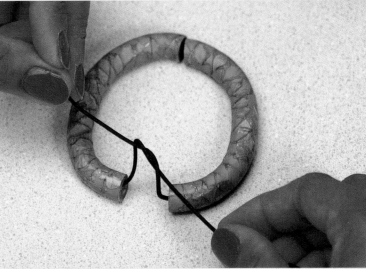

16. Trim Ends

Trim the elastic ends flush with the knot. Hide the knot inside the bracelet by pushing it into the larger hole with a needle tool. Superglue the knot in place. Position the bracelet around the perimeter of a glass jar, can or other round object to hold it open while the glue dries. This prevents the bracelet from accidentally being glued shut.

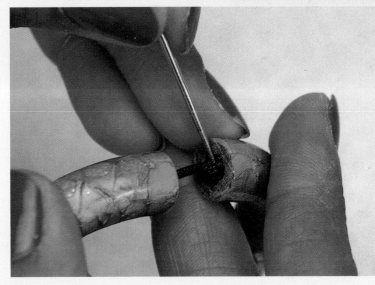

Mudcloth Pendant

Mudcloth, or bogolanfini, is made by the Bamana people of Mali in West Africa. Using sticks and small iron tools, they painted fermented mud onto handwoven cotton fabric. The unpainted areas represent symbolic patterns and suggestions of written script.

My goal was to imitate some of these patterns in this project, and I found that simple construction can have the appearance of complexity. Make this pendant "dance" with cowrie shell dangles! But don't be fooled — this faux vessel was not designed to open.

MATERIALS

- 2 blocks of beige polymer clay; I mixed 1 block of white + 1 block of champagne (Fimo Classic)
- 3 blocks of brown polymer clay; I mixed 1¹/₂ blocks black + 1¹/₂ blocks terra cotta (Fimo Classic)
- three 3" (7.6cm) eye pins
- four cowrie shells
- three beads with 2mm holes
- necklace cord
- clasp
- heavy-duty aluminum foil
- superglue gel
- pasta machine
- acrylic roller
- tissue blade
- needle tool
- wire cutters
- needle-nose pliers
- purse pattern (page 123)

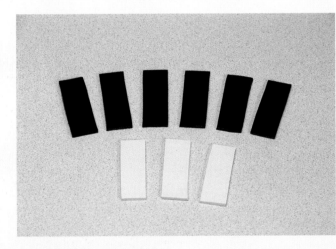

1. Cut Out Clay Strips

Condition 2 blocks of beige clay and 3 blocks of brown clay, and run each through the pasta machine on the #1 setting. With the tissue blade, cut three strips of beige clay and six strips of brown clay, each measuring 1¹/₄" x 3" (3.2cm x 7.6cm). Set the excess clay aside for later use.

2. Stack Strips

Stack the strips in the following order to create a cane: one brown, one beige, two brown, one beige, two brown, one beige, one brown.

3. Wrap Bar
Cut the remaining brown clay to the width of the striped cane. Wrap the clay around the cane and trim off the excess. Smooth the seam with your finger.

4. Reduce Cane
Reduce the cane to approximately 15" (38cm) long by pulling, stretching and rolling equally on all sides with an acrylic roller. Cut in half and set one half aside.

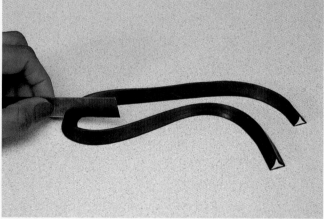

5. Wrap Triangle
Use some of the remaining beige clay to make a snake 1" (3cm) in diameter and 2" (5cm) long. Pinch the snake into a triangle. Trim the remaining brown sheet to the size of the triangle, wrap around and trim off excess. Smooth the seam with your finger.

6. Reduce Triangle
Reduce the triangle cane to approximately 17" (43cm), keeping the triangular shape. Cut in half and set one half aside.

7. Prepare Triangular Cane

Run the remaining brown clay through the pasta machine on the #4 setting. Wrap the clay around the triangular cane and trim off the excess. Smooth the seam with your finger. Cut into four equal pieces and combine the triangles into a square cane. Reduce to approximately 11" (28cm), working all four sides equally.

8. Prepare Remaining Clay

Run the remaining brown clay through the pasta machine on the #3 setting to make a strip 11" (28cm) long. To make a long strip, fold the clay lengthwise before feeding it into the machine. Place the entire cane on the brown strip and trim it flush against the edge. This is called a "pad."

9. Cut and Sandwich Cane

Cut the cane into four equal pieces and sandwich them together with a pad between each layer. Set aside for later use.

10. Reduce and Wrap Again

Reduce the striped cane from step 4 to approximately 11" (28cm). Trim the ends. Like in step 8, run the remaining brown piece through the pasta machine on the #1 setting. Place the cane block sideways on the sheet and trim flush with the edges to make another pad.

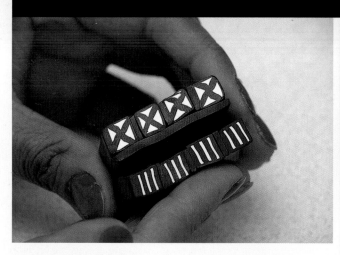

11. Adhere Clay Pad
Sandwich the pad between the two cane blocks to separate the striped and triangular designs. Press together and smooth the edges with your finger.

12. Adhere Another Pad
Make another pad and adhere it to the bottom of the block. Cut the entire block in half with a tissue blade.

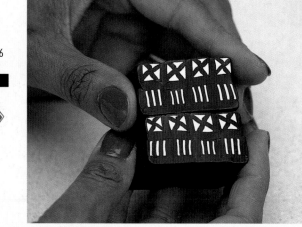

13. Stack Blocks
Stack the blocks, alternating the patterns. Make one more pad and adhere it to the other side of the block. Tidy up the outside edges with an acrylic roller. You now have a "complex cane."

14. Cut Slices from Cane
Cut four $\frac{1}{8}$" (3mm) slices from the complex cane. Align the slices end to end, smoothing the seams with your finger.

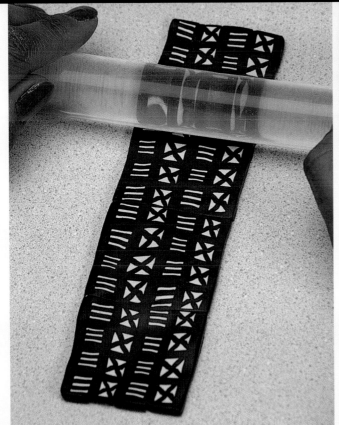

15. Remove Air Pockets
Press lightly with an acrylic roller to push out air pockets and even the surface.

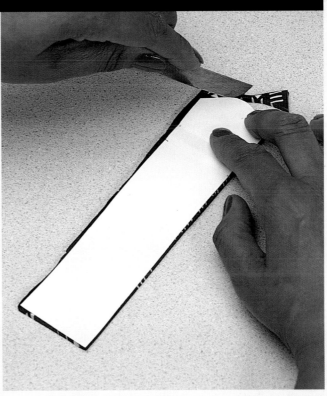

16. Cut Out Purse Shape
Cut out the purse pattern on page 123 and place it over the sheet. Cut around the edges with a tissue blade.

17. Shape Purse
Fold the purse pattern along the dotted lines to make a box. Crumple enough aluminum foil to fill the inside of the box.

18. Pierce Holes for Dangles
Place the crumpled foil on the clay sheet. Wrap the clay around the foil, mimicking the folds on the pattern. Pierce three holes at the base, about 1/4" (6mm) apart, with a needle tool. Bake for 15 minutes at 275° F (135° C). Allow to cool.

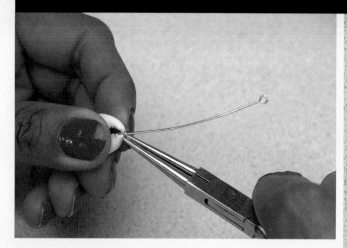

19. Prepare Dangles

Cut three 3" (8cm) eye pins in half with wire cutters. Bend loops in each of the straight pieces of wire and hook a cowrie shell on each loop. Use needle-nose pliers to bend the ends upward and twist the short ends around the long ends to secure the shells. Add beads to cover the twisted wire.

20. Make More Beads

Make three small beads from brown scrap clay and slide them over the remaining wire pieces until they rest against the eye.

21. Adhere Dangles

Place a few dots of superglue in the holes on the bottom of the purse. Slide the raw clay bead eye pins into the holes until they meet the glue.

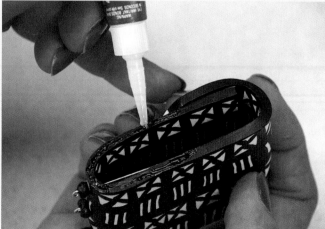

22. Make Purse Sides

To make the sides of the purse, cut one 1/8" (3mm) slice from the complex cane. Cut the slice in half with the tissue blade. Apply superglue to the open edges of the purse where the sides will be.

23. Add Purse Sides

Press the baked purse firmly against the raw side pieces and allow to dry for 20 seconds. Trim the edges flush against the purse.

24. Add Embellishments

To embellish the purse, roll a scrap of beige clay into a thin snake and superglue it onto the edge of the flap. Trim off the excess. Continue to add the beige trim where desired. Press a cowrie shell on a pad of beige clay and superglue it onto the flap for a faux clasp. Bake for 30 minutes at 275° F (135° C).

25. Finish Pendant

Trim the cowrie shell dangle wires to ¼" (6mm). Bend each wire into a loop with needle-nose pliers. Attach the dangles to the purse and close the loops with the pliers. To finish the pendant, string an extra long cord through the purse flap. Apply superglue to the inside of the flap to secure. Add a clasp or tie as desired.

Tip

To make a set of matching earrings, cut four thin slices from the mudcloth cane (two for each earring). Follow steps 16-22 on pages 94-95 to attach the French hook ear wires.

Bengal Tiger Brooch

I got the idea for this Bengal tiger cane after designing a zebra cane. Using a multi-colored blend for the background mimics the actual coloring of the tiger's coat.

For a variation, use gold clay with black stripes for a regular tiger cane. You can also try this technique for a zebra cane, using black and white.

MATERIALS

- ¹/₂ block of medium orange polymer clay; I mixed ¹/₄ block of orange + ¹/₄ block of champagne (Fimo Classic)

- ¹/₂ block of medium brown polymer clay; I mixed ¹/₄ block of terra cotta + ¹/₄ block of champagne (Fimo Classic)

- ¹/₂ block of beige polymer clay; I mixed ¹/₄ block of white + ¹/₄ block of champagne (Fimo Classic)

- 2 blocks of black polymer clay (Fimo Classic)

- liquid polymer clay (Translucent Liquid Sculpey [TLS])

- 1¹/₄" (0.6cm) pin back

- coarse sandpaper

- superglue

- pasta machine

- acrylic roller

- tissue blade

- paintbrush

- craft knife

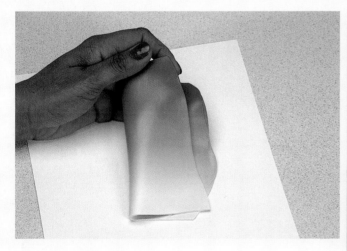

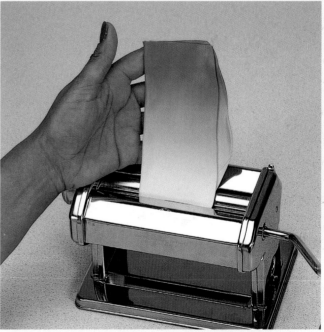

1. Prepare Blended Clay
Make a rainbow blend using medium orange, medium brown and beige clay (for instructions, see pages 18–19). Run the finished sheet through the pasta machine on the #3 setting. Fold the prepared clay sheet in half with the same colors touching.

2. Stretch Clay
Run the sheet through the pasta machine, lightest color first, on the #1, #3, #4, #5 and #6 settings. The clay will stretch into a long, thin sheet.

Tip

When you're rolling very long sheets of clay, it helps to have an extra set of hands to help you hold the clay as it gets longer.

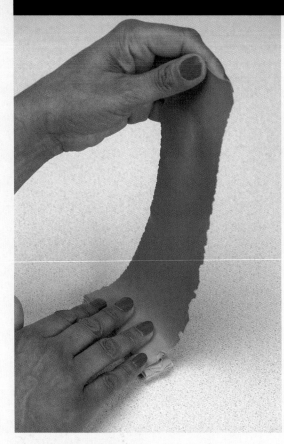

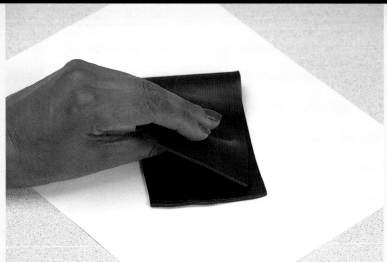

4. Fold Clay Sheet
Condition 2 blocks of black clay and set half aside for later use. Run the remaining clay through the pasta machine on the #2 setting. Fold the sheet in half so that the short ends are touching and trim the edges with a tissue blade.

3. Accordion-Fold Sheet
Hold the long strip up vertically and anchor the lightest end to the work surface. Accordion-fold the sheet about 1¼" (3cm) wide, creasing and pushing out air pockets as you go. Continue until the entire strip is folded. Straighten the edges with an acrylic roller and shape it into a bar measuring 1¼" x 3" (3cm x 8cm). Set aside for later use.

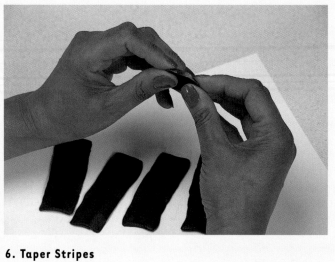

5. Cut Out Stripes
Use a tissue blade to cut the clay into several "stripes." Use a rectangular piece of cardboard as a template for even widths. Or, for natural-looking animal stripes, cut random widths, making sure that some are thinner than others.

6. Taper Stripes
Taper the long ends of each stripe with your fingers or a roller.

7. Depress Grooves

Use a paintbrush handle, knitting needle or other mandrel to randomly depress grooves into some of the stripes.

8. Cut Slices From Bar

Retrieve the colored bar from step 3 and stand it up on end with the darkest side facing to the right. Bow the tissue blade and slice straight down from top to bottom near one edge.

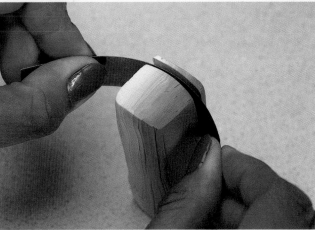

9. Position Stripes

Place one black stripe against the cut side of the blended bar, then place another slice. Repeat the process of slicing from the bar and sandwiching black stripes between slices.

113

Tip

Move your head from side to side to get a better view as you slice pieces from a bar. This maneuver helps you get a straighter, more even slice.

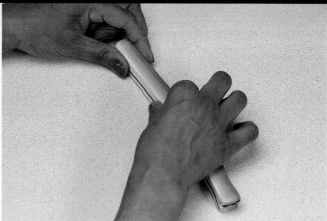

10. Vary Pattern

To vary the pattern, slice the colored bar at an angle toward the closest black stripe. Add another black stripe and compress to form a V-shaped stripe.

11. Reduce Cane

Reduce the cane to approximately 14" (36cm) by pulling, stretching and rolling the clay with an acrylic roller. Work both ends and all sides evenly. Trim about ½" (1cm) from each end.

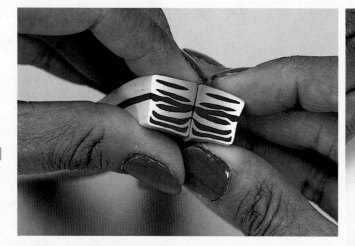

12. Cut and Stack Cane

Use a tissue blade to cut the cane in half. Place the pieces side by side, lining the striped patterns up in a mirror image. Cut and stack the cane again and compress it to make all the sides even.

13. Cut Slice and Flatten

Cut a slice ⅛" (3mm) thick from the cane and flatten it with an acrylic roller to spread the pattern. Position the slice in the pasta machine with the stripes running horizontally and run it through on the #1 setting. Trim the edges to the pattern with a craft knife. Bake for 15 minutes at 275° F (135° C). Allow to cool.

14. Prepare Clay for Border

To make a border for the brooch, run the remaining black clay from step 5 through the pasta machine on the #1 setting. Make sure the sheet is at least 1/4" (6mm) larger than the baked piece on all sides. Place the baked brooch on the raw clay.

15. Adhere Border

Trim around the edges of the brooch with a craft knife and remove the inside piece of raw clay. Drop the brooch into the hole and push the raw clay against it to seal the edges. Trim the edges to the border shape that you desire, bowing the tissue blade if necessary.

16. Texture Clay and Add Pin Back

Texture the clay with sandpaper or the material of your choice. Bake for 15 minutes at 275° F (135° C). Allow to cool. To finish the piece, use scraps of black clay to make the back of the brooch and adhere it with TLS. Superglue a pin back to the upper third of the piece. Cover the pin back with thin cane slices or an extra sheet of clay. Bake for 30 minutes at 275° F (135° C). Allow to cool.

Sea Turtle Pendant

Looking for other animal print canes to teach led me to books on sea turtles. Their colorful patterns remind me of splashes of paint on canvas. I attempted to imitate some of these patterns.

In this interesting cane, I have used the splicing technique to create splashes of color. Try this circular motif, or rearrange this cane to make a patterned grid.

MATERIALS

- ½ block of peach polymer clay; I mixed ¼ block of terra cotta + ¼ block of champagne (Fimo Classic)

- ½ block each of terra cotta, ochre, golden yellow and green polymer clay (Fimo Classic)

- ½ block of fluorescent yellow polymer clay (Fimo Soft)

- ⅛ block of light turquoise polymer clay (Fimo Classic)

- liquid polymer clay (Translucent Liquid Sculpey [TLS])

- 2mm leather cord

- necklace cord clasp

- aluminum foil

- superglue

- pasta machine

- acrylic roller

- tissue blade

- craft knife

- paintbrush

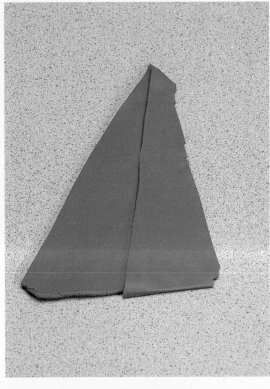

1. Make Double Triangles
Condition ½ block each of six contrasting colors (the colors I used are listed above) and run through the pasta machine on the #1 setting. Make strips measuring 2" x 5½" (5cm x 14cm). Cut the strips diagonally lengthwise with a tissue blade. Flip one half over so that both triangle bases are at the bottom as shown. This will make six double triangles.

2. Prepare and Accordion-Fold Sheets
Make two rainbow blends with the following colors, ordered from darkest to lightest: terra cotta, ochre and peach; and green, golden yellow and fluorescent yellow. Cut the blended sheets into thirds through all colors and stack the strips on top of each other with like colors touching. Taper the lightest narrow end of each sheet with an acrylic roller and run each sheet through the pasta machine, tapered-end first, on the #1, #3 and #4 settings without folding the clay. This will produce long, thin sheets. Accordion-fold each sheet, starting with the light end, and form into rectangular bars with an acrylic roller. You may need an extra set of hands to help with the holding and folding (see tip on page 111).

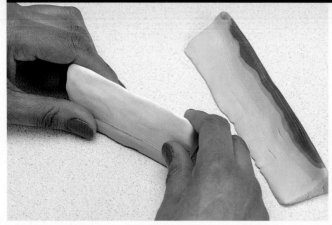

3. Pinch Bars Into Wedges

Pinch the lightest edge of each bar into a pointed wedge. Place the clay on the edge of a table and roll it with an acrylic roller at a 45° angle. Reduce both wedges to approximately 2" x 6" (5cm x 15cm) by pulling, stretching and rolling the clay.

4. Cut and Stack Wedges

Cut each wedge into four equal pieces. Stack the pieces together, alternating colors from each wedge. Place the narrow point of each wedge about 1/8" (3mm) from the edge.

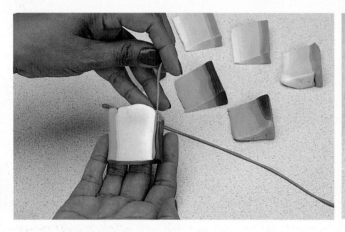

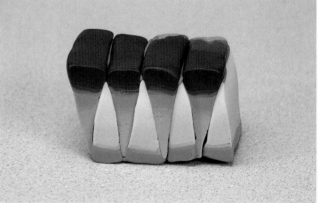

5. Add Snakes to Wedges

Roll a thin snake out of conditioned turquoise clay. Place small pieces of the snake at the end of the wedges. Do this on both sides.

6. Reduce, Cut and Combine Wedge

Continue layering and adding snakes on both sides until all eight wedges are used. This process is called "splicing." Pinch one end of the cane into a wedge and reduce to about 9" (23cm). Trim the ends and cut the wedge into thirds. Combine the three pieces, keeping like colors together.

7. Form Semicircle

Cut the stack in half with a tissue blade and combine the pieces to form a semicircle. Smooth the seam with your finger.

8. Form Circle

Cut the semicircle in half and put the halves together to form a circle. Cut a 1/4" (6mm) slice from the circle and level the slice with an acrylic roller.

9. Position Slice in Dome Shape

Crumple a piece of aluminum foil into a dome shape. Place the slice on the foil and press the sides down to conform to the dome shape. You could also use a light bulb or the bottom of a smooth bowl to shape the dome. Bake for 20 minutes at 275° F (135° C). Allow to cool.

10. Prepare Pendant Back

To make the back of your pendant, condition the remainder of the terra cotta clay and run it through the pasta machine on the #1 setting. Using a paintbrush, apply TLS to the inside lip of the baked piece and compress it into the raw clay. Trim the edges with a craft knife.

11. Make Border

Use the terra cotta clay scraps to roll out a snake long enough to wrap around the edge of the pendant. Press against the raw clay to adhere.

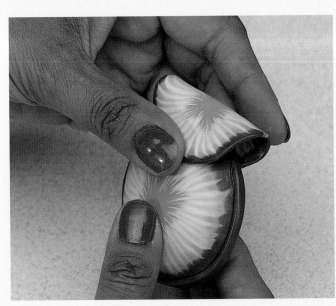

12. Finish Pendant

Reduce the original cane and cut a slice about 1/8" (3mm) thick. Fold in half. Add dots of superglue to the top of the baked piece on the front and back. Adhere the folded slice. Bake 30 minutes at 275° F (135° C). Allow to cool. String a leather cord through the curved shell and fasten a clasp or tie as desired.

Tip

Mini versions of this pendant make great earrings. Reduce the cane by pulling, stretching and rolling it to the desired size. Cut two slices from the cane (one for each earring) and use leftover brown clay to make backs similar to the pendant. Follow steps 18-22 on pages 94-95 to attach French hook ear wires.

Canes Gallery

Bengal Tiger Vessel Pendant
To make this beautiful vessel, I mounted several cane slices onto a base sheet of clay. The patterned sheet was baked on an armature made of heavy paper. I cut the lid when it was still warm out of oven, and baked a lip inside the lid to prevent it from slipping. Finally, I strung a leather cord through drilled holes for the perfect hanging vessel.

Leaf-covered Cowrie Shell Necklace
Here, I embedded a large cowrie shell on a base sheet of clay and surrounded it with leaf canes made of translucent and beige clays. The leaf canes continue to form the bail, or looped support to hold the cord.

Leaf Cane Brooch
I mixed black and white embossing powders into the clay before constructing these leaf canes. The canes were reduced into several different sizes, sliced, then layered onto a base sheet of clay for added dimension.

Sand Dollar Necklace Set

I USED THE SPLICING TECHNIQUE TO CREATE THIS SAND DOLLAR CANE FOR THIS MATCHING SET. GLOW-IN-THE-DARK CLAY ILLUMINATES THESE PIECES WHEN THE LIGHTS GO OUT! I EMBEDDED THE NECKLACE WITH AFRICAN BRASS AND FRESHWATER PEARLS.

Animal Print Brooches

I DESIGNED THESE TIGER, ZEBRA AND LEOPARD CANES TO REPRESENT PATTERNS OF ANIMAL FUR. A SLICE WAS CUT FROM EACH CANE, BAKED, SANDED AND LIGHTLY BUFFED. I ADDED BLACK CLAY BORDERS TO FINISH THE BROOCHES. TO TAKE THE DESIGN A STEP FURTHER, I LIKE TO TEXTURE THE BACKS OF MY PENDANTS WITH WITH PLASTIC MESH, THEN APPLY BRIGHTLY COLORED LEAF CANES TO COVER THE PIN BACKS. A QUICK BAKING AND THEY'RE READY TO WEAR!

Patterns

Following are patterns for some of the projects in this book. Trace these onto a piece of paper and cut out, then use the cut-out as a guide when cutting your clay. All the templates are shown here at full size.

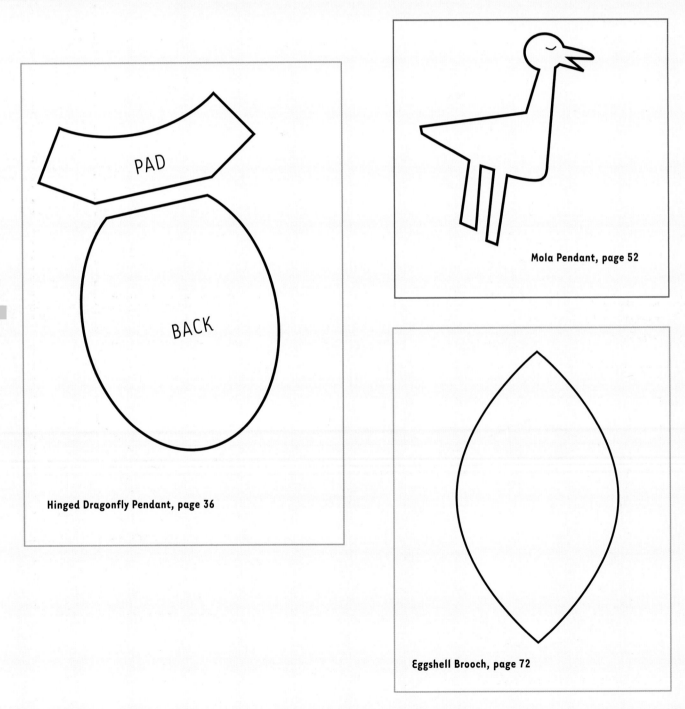

PAD

BACK

Hinged Dragonfly Pendant, page 36

Mola Pendant, page 52

Eggshell Brooch, page 72

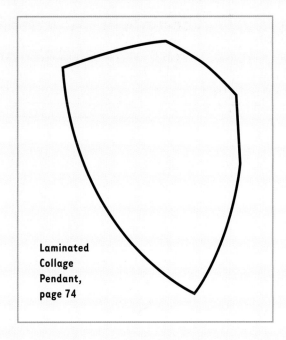

Laminated
Collage
Pendant,
page 74

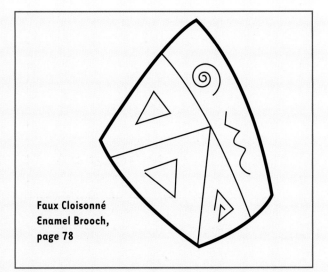

Faux Cloisonné
Enamel Brooch,
page 78

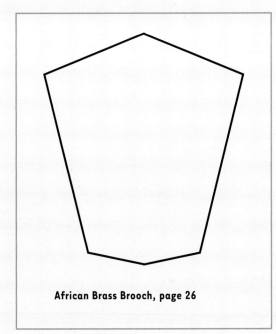

African Brass Brooch, page 26

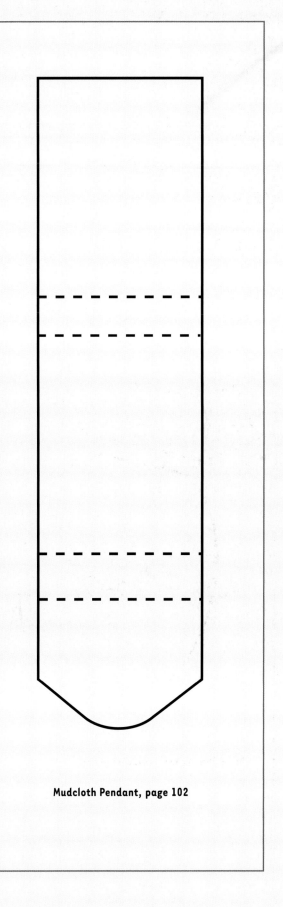

Mudcloth Pendant, page 102

123

RESOURCES

Most of the materials and supplies used in this book are readily available through art and craft stores, hobby stores, or polymer clay specialty stores and beading shops. If you have difficulty locating any of these materials, below are manufacturers that will be able to direct you to a supplier in your area.

American Plastic Distributors, Inc.

1015 West Fifth Avenue
Columbus, Ohio 43212
(614) 294-5100
Fax: (614) 294-5103
Acrylic rollers, sheets

Creative Claystamps

www.claystamp.com
bmcguire@claystamp.com
Clay stamps, templates

Harold Import Company, Inc.

747 Vassar Avenue
Lakewood, New Jersey 08701-4588
(800) 526-2163
Fax: (732) 364-3253
www.haroldskitchen.com
Pasta machines, motors, cookie cutters

I.B. Moore Company ,Inc.

648 Laco Drive
Lexington, Kentucky 40510
(800) 335-7899
Fax: (859) 254-4389
www.ibmoore.com
Assorted sizes of Buna rubber cord

Prizm Artist's Supply Store

1270 East Powell Road
Lewis Center, Ohio 43035
(614) 841-4540
Fax: (614) 841-4086
www.prizmart.com
Polymer clay, tools and artist supplies

Rings & Things

P.O. Box 450
Spokane, Washington 99201-0450
(800) 366-2156
www.rings-things.com
Quality jewelry findings, beads and supplies

Rio Grande

7500 Bluewater Road NW
Albuquerque, New Mexico 87121
(800) 545-6566
www.riogrande.com
Jewelry supplies, findings, sterling wire

Thomas Scientific

P.O. Box 99
Swedesboro, New Jersey 08085-0099
(800) 345-2100
Fax: (800) 345-5232
www.thomassci.com
Surgical steel tissue blades

Van Aken International

9157 Rochester Court
P.O. Box 1680
Rancho Cucamonga, California 91729
(909) 980-2001
Fax: (909) 980-2333
www.vanaken.com and
www.katopolyclay.com
Kato Polyclay Clear Medium, polymer clay, tools

There's a wealth of information about polymer clay available. Following are a few of my favorite books and magazines. And consider joining a polymer clay group in your area—they're a wonderful way to share your enthusiasm with others.

Books

Foundations in Polymer Clay Design

Barbara McGuire
Iola, Wisconsin
Krause Publications, 1999

The New Clay: Techniques and Approaches to Jewelry Making

Nan Roche
Rockville, Maryland
Flower Valley Press, 1991

Polymer Clay: Creating Functional and Decorative Objects

Jacqueline Gikow
Iola, Wisconsin
Krause Publications, 2001

The Polymer Clay Techniques Book

Sue Heaser
Cincinnati, Ohio
North Light Books, 1999

Polymer: The Chameleon Clay

Victoria Hughes
Iola, Wisconsin
Krause Publications, 2002

Periodicals

Belle Armoire: Art to Wear

(877) STAMPER
www.bellearmoire.com
Quarterly magazine featuring
artistic handmade clothing,
jewelry and accessories

The Crafts Report

(800) 777-7098
www.craftsreport.com
Monthly magazine for the
business crafter

Expression:Sharing the Spirit of Creative Arts

(619) 819-4520
www.expressionartmagazine.com
Bimonthly magazine featuring polymer clay, paper arts, art books and
home décor

Ornament

(800) 888-8950
ornament@cts.com
Quarterly magazine promoting the
richness and diversity of jewelry,
clothing and beads

PolymerCAFÉ

(678) 380-5783
www.polymercafe.com
Quarterly magazine dedicated to
delivering the latest news,
instruction and events to professional artists, crafters and
enthusiasts in polymer clay

Organizations

National Polymer
Clay Guild
www.npcg.org
An organization promot-
ing an interest in the use
of polymer clay as an
artistic medium

Ohio Designer Craftsmen

(614) 486-4402
www.ohiocraft.org
An organization that promotes a
standard of excellence in crafts and
encourages creative growth and support to professional artists

INDEX

126

The best polymer clay projects come from North Light Books!

Creative Stamping in Polymer Clay

Filled with fresh designs, simple techniques and gorgeous colors, this exciting book combines two fun, easy-to-master crafts in one. You'll find guidelines for stamping images on all your clay creations, including jewelry, home décor and more, along with advice for experimenting with color and finish. The wide variety of projects guarantees spontaneous, delightful results.

ISBN 1-58180-155-6
paperback, 128 pages
#31904-K

Creative Home Décor in Polymer Clay

Now you can use polymer clay to create elegant designs for your home! Nineteen step-by-step projects make getting started easy. You'll learn how to combine clay with fabric, silverware and other household items, plus metallic powders that simulate colored glass, antique bronze or gleaming silver. You'll also find instructions for color mixing, marbling and caning.

ISBN 1-58180-139-4
paperback, 128 pages
#31880-K

Rubber Stamped Jewelry

Create fabulous jewelry with simple techniques for beautiful results. In no time at all, readers will learn invaluable methods to create lovely earrings, necklaces, bracelets and brooches using a wide array of easy-to-find materials like fabric, paper, polymer clay and, of course, rubber stamps. Guided by easy-to-follow instructions, crafters will find just how easy it is to fashion truly breathtaking and unique jewelry and gifts.

ISBN 1-58180-384-2
paperback, 128 pages
#32415-K

Polymer Clay Extravaganza

Fast and fun this book features 20 dazzling projects that combine easy polymer clay techniques with a variety of accessible mediums, including mosaic, wire stamping, foiling, millefiore, caning and metal embossing. Step-by-step instructions, full color photos and a section for beginners guarantees success. This unique guide also includes an inspiring idea gallery that encourages crafters to expand their creativity and develop original pieces of their own.

ISBN 1-58180-188-2
paperback, 128 pages
#31960-K

These and other fine North Light titles are available from your local art & craft retailer, bookstore, online supplier or by calling 1-800-448-0915.